CW00881062

UNDERSTANDING THE SEASONS OF LIFE

JOKÉ SOLANKÉ

UNDERSTANDING THE SEASONS OF LIFE

iUniverse books may be ordered through booksellers or by contacting:

iUniverse
1663 Liberty Drive
Bloomington, IN 47403
www.iuniverse.com
1-800-Authors (1-800-288-4677)

ISBN: 978-1-5320-6932-1 (sc)
ISBN: 978-1-5320-6934-5 (hc)
ISBN: 978-1-5320-6933-8 (e)

Library of Congress Control Number: 2019902772

Print information available on the last page.

iUniverse rev. date: 03/12/2019

CONTENTS

PREFACE

I t was my favorite season of the year; the leaves were falling off the trees, and the harsh summer weather was giving way to a cooler and more refreshing season. As I stood by the window in my room to ponder about life and the people I have encountered on my journey, it dawned on me that everything about life is seasonal—change is permanent!

Although we prepare for seasonal changes, which are easily predictable, many do not have enough understanding to handle the changes in the seasons of life as they come their way, probably due to the unpredictability of what seems like certain life events. I have not encountered anyone who chose to tie the nuptial knot with an agreement to divorce in place at the time of the wedding ceremony.

We have a formal educational system to equip people for career and trades, which are a fractional part of life; however; there seems to be no system in place to prepare for "real" life. Many have made costly and irreversible decisions based on a life experience that was for only a season. I have been privileged to have access to people's lives in a diverse way. I started my career teaching high school mathematics before changing to nursing. I have worked with numerous patients in both inpatient and outpatient settings in different specialties, led youth groups and women's groups, served as a pioneer member of a church organization in at least two countries, and managed multiple healthcare clinics, with the responsibility of coaching, mentoring, and providing professional development guidance for my teams.

The encounters I had relating with people at a grassroots level exposed me to three categories of people (based on their level of formal education): illiterates, semi-illiterates, and literates. It is interesting to note that formal education does not prepare anyone for dealing with the complexities of life. I have seen people deemed to be 'uneducated' deal with crisis and life changes with aptitude and educated people crumble under the weight of life's adversities. Many have made decisions based on where they are and their current life experience without factoring in imminent, inevitable life changes. Understanding life experience as a seasonal event helps provide the fortitude to endure seasons that may not be pleasant.

I do not like the winter, but I endure the unpleasant feelings, because I have hope that eventually, winter will give way to spring. I have also learned to appreciate winter because of the purpose it has to serve, although I don't look forward to it. Similarly, when you see life as a season, you are equipped with hope. You expect a change in the not-so-pleasant situation you may be in, and you appreciate the purpose and benefit of your experience. Every season has its own benefits, and such is life.

Life seasons are unique to each individual. You may experience all four seasons simultaneously, while your friend may only have to deal with one season of pleasant experience despite common goals, commitments, and investment of time, talent, and treasure. Your life experience may be different from mine, but the process of life is the same.

We all know the basics about life; however, knowledge is not enough. What is the use of information you cannot comprehend? Understanding is the bridge between what you know and how to apply it. You can never apply information you do not comprehend. This book will provide the knowledge you need to navigate your path through the maze of life and help you find meaning in every situation and circumstance.

CHAPTER 1

THE CONSTANCY OF CHANGE

There are two ways to experience change: you can change before you have to or change because you have to.

To delve into the subject of life seasons, we need to understand the fundamentals of change. Every season is unique and evolves through a change experience that comes naturally, with or without preparation. Change is one of the most consistent life events. Nothing in life remains the same forever—neither your body nor your relationships nor your family dynamics. Life cannot exist without change; it is a sign of existence. With change comes opportunities or challenges, depending on individual perspectives, orientation, and beliefs. Change can make you either grow or groan; it can reform you or deform you. Every change will present with a form of crisis, including positive change, since there will be an alteration in your normal routine and the birthing of something new and foreign to your established pattern of life. Your problem-solving abilities will determine your chance at getting a benefit out of the changes that you encounter on your life path. Irrespective of the inevitable challenges embedded in the journey of life, it is possible to have a good outlook during every season, regardless of the changes and attending trials that come with these changes.

Understanding the seasons of life requires you accept the reality of "change." No matter how much you detest and resist change, it remains unavoidable. Nature clearly emphasizes the certainty of change through various seasons—cold and heat, winter and summer, day and night, seedtime and harvest. Everything around echoes the constant state of change, from conception to death. Every man will experience metamorphosis at every stage of life. You will continue to evolve! Your life experience is not unique. It is common. However, the way you deal with your experience is peculiar to you and your level of understanding. Everyone will have a taste of sweet and sour, either concurrently or at different times throughout life's pilgrimage. Your uniqueness lies in the way you handle your experience.

The world system keeps changing and will continue to evolve. Technological advancement is not what it was five decades ago, and it will not be the same in the next five decades. Things are bound to change. How do you cope with the ever-changing systems? How do you manage the changes in your personal life? You have the choice to either leave things to chance or prepare for change. Change brings about different seasons—some pleasant, some unpleasant. Every season of life, no matter how satisfying or otherwise, comes with a lesson, a blessing, a breakthrough, as well as opportunities that every man needs to evolve into purpose and destiny. In spite of the many potentials embedded in the various experience of life changes, many people lack the skills required to tap into the opportunities that come with change so they might profit. Some see opportunities in their adversity; others see stumbling blocks and hindrances instead of stepping stones. When you understand the seasons of life, it will be easy to know and accept that all things will eventually work together for the good, no matter how horrible the situation might be at the moment.

The seemingly "hopeless season" of a man's life can become the most fruitful if one understands the season and has the wisdom to tackle every attending adversity, turning it into gains.

> *Missteps and roadblocks are inevitable but are ultimately an opportunity to learn, pivot, and go after your goals with a new perspective.*
> —Jenny Fleiss

Many know change is needed in life but do not understand the purpose and benefits of change, and so they abuse, misuse, misappropriate, and underutilize the opportunities ingrained in the change that comes their way.

Understanding the different seasons of life positions people for effective optimization of the opportunities in each season. People who have been able to comprehend life's seasons are better equipped to take advantage of change when it presents itself instead of resisting it. The best way to handle change is to initiate it. You may tend to become a victim if you are passive instead of proactive about the happenings in your life and environment. There are two ways to experience change: you can change *before* you have to or change *because* you have to. You cannot stop change, but you have all you need to manage and control any and every situation that may present with the tendencies of altering your life. Effective management of change puts you at the cutting edge of life's events in a productive way. Change has the possibility of bringing either adversity or prosperity. Change can add value to or devalue your life.

No one is stagnant in life. Everyone will go through change, whether consciously or unconsciously. Have you thought about why there is a disparity in the outcome when two different individuals have similar circumstances? What makes one person handle or respond to a situation better than another person? Why do some people see results for their efforts, and some don't? It is all as a result of adequate or inadequate preparation for change. Your preparedness for the realities of the complexities of life, with its ever-changing seasons, puts you at an advantage over life's crises. Your current situation is not supposed to define you. If you see life as a puzzle, then you will understand that a piece of the puzzle can never make sense until the whole puzzle is put together. Your current situation is only an integral part of your life and will soon change for better or for worse, depending on you.

I read a story on Belief.net about the four seasons of a tree. The story has much relevance and is worth sharing. There was a man who wanted to teach his four sons the blessings that comes with seasonal change. He desired to instill in his sons the importance of not judging things too quickly. So, he had each of them embark on a trip, each at a different time, to observe a pear tree that was some distance away and report back their findings. He sent the first son in winter, the second son in spring, the third son in summer, and the last son during the fall. After all the trips ended, he called a meeting to have the sons report their findings.

The first son said that the tree looked ugly, twisted, with no sign of life. The second son had a different opinion; he said the tree looked beautiful, with green buds and the potential for fruitfulness. The third son had a different view; he said it was blossoming with fragrance. The last son's perspective was different still; he said it was ripe, lively, and drooping with fruit. The man then enlightened his sons that they were all accurate, since each son had seen only one season in the tree's life. He told them to avoid judging a tree, or an individual, by one season, and that the quintessence of who they are can only be measured at the end, when all the seasons are up. If you give up in winter, you stand the chance of missing the promise of your spring, the splendor of your summer, and the satisfaction of your fall.

> *Never allow the discomfort of one season to destroy the enjoyment of all the rest. Don't judge life by one challenging season. Persevere through the difficult patches, and better times are sure to come.*
> *—Author unknown*

Since change is inevitable, you must hone the skills you need to manage change effectively. A woman once told me how she had been laid off from work after three decades of dedicated service. Her position was no longer useful to the company, and since she had never prepared for the change by making herself relevant in other areas, she was forced to resign. Her lack of preparedness for change turned twenty-nine years of invested time and talent into a waste. When change is not initiated from within, the change without can overwhelm the structures you have put together. Change can turn years of labor and investment into nothing if you remain on the sideline.

I engaged a photographer in a conversation about the need to keep up with technology and the apparent change it has brought to the photography business. The response the individual gave me, as well as the person's disposition, was all I needed to predict his imminent failure and frustration in the photography business. Rigidity in the face of visible change around things that can affect your livelihood makes you a victim of change. You don't have to be able to change what is going on around you, but you should be able to change whatever is going on within you—and you have what it takes to change you!

The first step toward understanding the seasons of life is to accept the reality of change. The relationship that makes you excited today may bring depression tomorrow. The cute baby that you are showing off today may turn out to be a rebellious teenager, regardless of whether you have done everything right. The job or business you are bragging about now may go bankrupt.

There can be no life without change. The sign that you are alive is ingrained in the change you experience. Your survival in life will be determined by how you can handle change.

> *It is not the strongest of the species that survives, nor the most intelligent, but the one most responsive to change.*
>
> *—Charles Darwin*

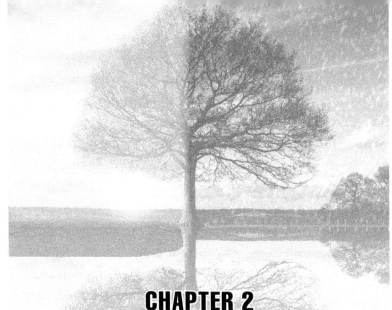

CHAPTER 2

THE AUTHOR OF LIFE

Your next prospect in life may be in a book that you have failed to create time to read.

Thorough knowledge and understanding of the Author of life is a prerequisite to coming to terms with certain realities. God owns the script to every person's life, and He understands everything about you and your frailty, including things you might not know about yourself. No matter how intelligent and strategic you are in life, certain things remain absolute and under the control of the one who fashioned life. For an in-depth understanding of life's season, it is very fundamental to be acquainted with the Author, the Architect, the Designer, and the Engineer of life. Since there are many things in life beyond the control of man, anyone who desires to understand life and its seasons must glean from the Author of life. Every product has a producer, and the best person who can show you how to use a product, fix a product, and define the originality of the product and its purpose is the manufacturer of that product, since every manufacturer has an intention for their products. God has a plan for all his creatures.

In the same way that many products are not being used or put together according to the manufacturer's intention, many people are not living their lives according to divine design. I have been guilty of trying to figure out how to assemble a product without consulting the accompanying manufacturer's instruction manual. Often, I get stuck in the middle of putting the product together despite a good start, and the only option left has always been to dismantle everything and start all over again. Initiating the assembling of a product is stress-free. The complications often arise somewhere midway or toward the end of completing the task. Is that not the same way we handle life? We don't realize our errors of making assumptions until later in life, for many, the damages may be irreparable.

Many people are on a quest of figuring life out without guidance and alliance with the Author of life. No wonder many are stuck and unfulfilled; the life they have created for themselves is incongruent with the script authored about them. I hope you have been able to make a personal discovery—that fulfillment in life has nothing to do with material acquisitions, academic excellence, beauty, fame, and all other worldly achievements.

I was privileged to engage a seventy-six-year-old man in a conversation recently. He lamented about missed opportunities in his life. Yes, he lived and did many brilliant things and was privileged to live long in good health; however, he had many regrets. It took him almost eight decades to discover his purpose. Unfortunately, time is no longer an advantage for him. I'd like you to pause, ponder, take inventory, and evaluate your life at this point. Does your career have any relevance to your purpose, or is it only a means of existence? Why do you do what you do? Do you have fulfillment and satisfaction in your life's quests and things that have engaged your time? Your honest response to the outlined questions may precipitate the need to take a detour from your current journey around existence and embark on an adventure toward the purpose of your life. Many have died a "potential," and they had everything they needed to become their authentic self in life, but they never discovered their unique purpose. They died struggling to be who they could never become.

> *We all want progress, but if you're on the wrong road,*
> *progress means doing an about-turn and walking*
> *back to the road; in that case, the man who turns*
> *back soonest is the most progressive.*
> —C. S. Lewis

Starting over may seem insane, especially in the face of apparent results and life's accomplishments. No matter how accomplished you are, based on societal standards, there is always a void in every life lived outside of purpose. The path to true fulfillment in life lies in the discovery and actualization of purpose. Until you plug yourself into "purpose," the void of dissatisfaction will remain in your life. No man has the true definition of his life. The Author of life does. The discovery of your natural talents is not synonymous to purpose. Talents are tools needed to actualize purpose. You may be gifted in music, playing different instruments, or singing. You may be a talented public speaker with impressive ability. Perhaps you are a nurturing individual with adept skills in teaching and coaching. The list of talents remains unending.

Whatever your talent is, there is the need to ask and answer the question: "Why do I do what I do?" Talents used outside of purpose can be destructive. Your natural abilities are to serve a purpose. When that purpose is unknown, misuse or abuse becomes obvious. I have seen many people destroyed in the course of engaging their talents for fame or gain at the expense of purpose. The confusing situation in many lives results from the lack of a guiding principle, and it is practically impossible to follow a principle that you do not know. Unfortunately, ignorance can never excuse a man from the consequences of his actions or inactions. Everyone needs to take an adventure toward the acquisition of knowledge and be "life smart." Many people are "book smart," with multiple accolades and achievements, but they are incompetent when it comes to handling life's crises.

God has authored life in such a way that His principles are set to work for anyone who follows them, irrespective of their faith or beliefs. To handle the challenges that accompany life's season, one must possess an in-depth understanding of established fundamentals instituted by the author of life that no man can change or influence. The ability to accept things that cannot change is the gateway to a life void of confusion and stress. Many are engaged in an endless venture to change things that cannot change at the expense of things that can.

I can imagine what was going on in the mind of Reinhold Niebuhr in 1943, when he wrote the serenity prayer: "God, give us the grace to accept with serenity the things that cannot be changed, courage to change the things that can be changed, and the wisdom to distinguish the one from the other."

There is no easy route in life; every man must go through moments of unpleasant realities that cannot be changed but endured.

It is essential for you to know the difference between what you can change and what you cannot change. As an individual, you must understand and accept your limitations, your responsibilities, and others' responsibilities. The ability to recognize and own up to your limits will keep you sane during seasons of inevitable crisis. Listed below are seven fundamental keys to understanding the mysteries of life so you will not lose your mind:

1. There are questions in life you cannot answer and will never be able to answer.
2. There are issues that you can never explain, regardless of how intelligent you think you are.
3. There are events you can never change, no matter how strategic or wise you think you are.
4. There are situations you can never control, no matter how powerful or influential you are.
5. There are things in life you cannot stop.
6. There are things in life you are not responsible for.
7. There are limitations in life you cannot remove

The Brevity of Life

One of the things a man cannot change is the length of his days. God has authored a timeline for everyone, and no man is created to live indefinitely on the face of the earth. There is a preset timeline for your life, and the only time you have and

can control is now. It is imperative that you own the moment—
now—and cease procrastinating, since tomorrow may never
come. You are not immortal, and you cannot negotiate with
death when it comes knocking at your door. In the face of
death, the strength of the mighty fails, the wisdom of the
noble becomes irrelevant, and the knowledge of the intellectual
becomes null and void. Riches, influence, position, and status
are not enough to bribe death. Death is a status equalizer. It
does not discriminate between the youth and the aged, the
educated and the illiterate, the ignoramus and the sage, the
pauper and the prince, the healthy and the sick—everybody is
the same in the face of death. It's only seeking to take just one
thing from everyone: breath!

> *How frail is humanity! How short is life, how full of
> trouble! We blossom like a flower and then wither.
> Like a passing shadow, we quickly disappear. Must
> you keep an eye on such a frail creature and demand
> an accounting from me? Who can bring purity out
> of an impure person? No one! You have decided the
> length of our lives. You know how many months we
> will live, and we do not have a minute longer.*
>
> —Job

The reality is that no man can predict how long he will
live. Neither can he know the where, when, and how of his
departure from the terrestrial. Regardless of your healthy
lifestyle and mindfulness, you will eventually die.

This truth should jolt you to reality and make you stand in
awe of the only one who can give life. The brevity of life also
calls for a need to redefine your priorities and reprioritize your
priorities. You cannot be all to all and all in all. I had to ask

myself this question: If today were to be my last day on earth, what would I have loved to do that I have not done? What sacrifice do I need to make to get "relevant" things done? Your answer to the above questions should help you set your life priorities and eliminate irrelevant things that have hampered and cluttered your life so you can engage in things that will give you fulfillment.

> *Every worthwhile venture will always demand a sacrifice.*

Your ability to define your priorities is an antidote to depression and a motivation to refocus on things that have relevance to your purpose. Often we are depressed over issues that have no connection to the script God has written for us, and we just deplete the resources and energy we need to live our God-ordained life.

> *For any one of us forever could end in an hour or a hundred years from now. You never know for sure, so you'd better make every second count.*
> —Sarah Dessen.

The understanding of the brevity of life and the inevitability of death should also help us embrace and cherish our loved ones, since we can never predict how long we have to spend together on the terrestrial. The most important thing you can give your loved ones is always going to be memories, not material things. It is very crucial that you create good memories for people around you. People can misplace or outgrow stuff you give them but will never forget the memories you leave with them.

What memories are you creating for the people around you? The memories you create for people will always outlive you.

My grandparents did not know that they were creating memories for their little granddaughter, memories that lingered after their demise. Both of them probably thought that they were living their normal life. Little did they know that I was watching and that the memories they left with me were so incredible. I have yet to see a marriage relationship as worthy of emulation as theirs. The expression of the love they shared, the mutual respect, the bond, the affection, the understanding, the transparency, the oneness, and factually everything about them was extraordinary! Whenever I am tempted to think that it is impossible to have a perfect marriage based on all that I see around, their memories have always helped me to see the possibility of building a healthy relationship—provided you are privileged to connect with the "right" person.

> *Cherish every moment and every person in your life, because you never know when it will be the last time you see someone.*
> *—Anonymous*

What memories have you created, or are you creating, about yourself? Grasping the truth about the brevity of life will help you tap into wisdom for life instead of being overly consumed by irrelevant issues.

I read the story about a rich man, Job, who lost all his investments, his ten children, business empire, and his health overnight. He reflected on the sudden loss of all that he had labored for and exclaimed, "Teach us to realize the brevity of life, so that we may grow in wisdom."

The Concept of Time

One resource every man possesses indiscriminately is time. Your greatest asset in life is not your money or degree and pedigree; it is time. If you do not know the value of time and its implication to your life, you can never grasp the understanding of life's seasons. Time is more powerful than money. It is the legal tender for the earth's economic transactions. You have to sell your time to make money. The value you have added to your life over time will determine the worth of your time. The quality of your life is directly proportional to how you invest in time. It makes perfect sense to say, "Time is more valuable than money." Every human, regardless of race, gender, geographical location, or educational status, has an equivalent amount of time each day: 86,400 seconds. Time is one asset you cannot afford to let other people control. The people or anything you allow to manage your time are actually in control of your life, since the accumulation of your time overtime will equate to your life. Time, as it were, can be engaged by man, consciously or unconsciously, and each person has the autonomy to decide the utilization of their time. Men of understanding make a conscious decision on the allocation of their time.

The way you engage your time will overtime determine your worth in life.

You can make your time count and valuable. You can decide to spend time or invest in time. You can use your time or abuse your time. You can be careless with your time and allow others to steal time away from you. You can waste, squander, or lose time. God has created time for everything, and if you don't grasp the understanding of the concept of divine timing, you can do a wrong thing at the wrong time, a right thing at the wrong time, a wrong thing at the right time, or a right thing at the right time. The timing of your actions will ultimately determine the appreciation or depreciation of the value of your life. When you fail to engage your time wisely, you will eventually fail in life. It will be beneficial for you to take an inventory of how you are currently using your time. Are you spending your time on things that have relevance to your life's purpose? Are what you engage your time in adding value to your life over time? It will be beneficial for you to appropriate your time based on your life's purpose and priorities. Unfortunately, if you are yet to discover your purpose and define what is paramount in your life, the only thing that you can do with your time is squander it or use it to help build other people's dreams. The way you spend every second will translate to how you spend your day, your week, your months, your years, and eventually your life.

What consumes your time? Your response to this question may be all you need to set things straight in your life, for there is time for everything. Your achievements, education, skills, or people you know will never be sufficient for your sustenance in life if you miss your time.

> *I have observed something else under the sun. The fastest runner doesn't always win the race, and the strongest warrior doesn't always win the battle. The wise sometimes go hungry, and the skillful are not necessarily wealthy. And those who are educated don't always lead successful lives. It is all decided by chance, by being in the right place at the right time.*
> *—King Solomon*

Every breaking of the day presents with new opportunities, and some are meant to be life-changing. When you start your day without expectations, goals, or aspirations, it will be impossible to tap into opportunities that come your way. Your next prospect in life may be in a book that you have failed to create time to read. It may be a volunteer activity that will help people discover your competencies or attending a conference that will connect you with bright minds. You need to be intentional about your daily expedition and also set expectations that will yield measurable results that account for the investment of your time. It is beneficial to have a system of reflection in place that will help you evaluate how you have invested your time each day with the identification of missed opportunities, wasted time, and plans to avoid known pitfalls. Your time is your life!

The Concept of Choice

Another predetermined life principle is the concept of choice. It is a critical concept because the seasons of our life depend on the choices we make. The choices you make in life can create adversity or prosperity. Please understand that adversity or prosperity is not a function of money. Financial strength is an integral part of prosperity. You can be financially buoyant and have ill health or relationships and other life issues that money cannot solve. You have the willpower and intellectual capabilities you need to create your world. You are ultimately responsible for deciding the happenings in your life. It does not matter what others are doing or what the environment is saying; you have the power to choose what your life will become.

Only you can determine the "quality" of your life!

There are certain things no one will ever choose for you. You have been endowed with enough intellectual and creative capabilities to recreate and redesign your life any way you want it. Never give the power of your life's choice to anyone, especially people who do not know or understand your purpose. It is time for you to quit blaming others for your woes and take ownership of your life by giving it whatever is required to redesign your life the way you want it to be.

There is an old story of two twin brothers that speaks loudly to the concept of choice and individual accountability. One of the twins was a drunkard, and the other was not. The drunkard was questioned on why he ended up an alcohol addict, and the other one was asked what helped him to stay away from alcohol. It was fascinating that they both presented with the same reason—their alcoholic father. One chose not to go through the experience and consequences of alcoholism, based on what he saw in his father. The other one chose to pattern his life after his alcoholic father.

No one is responsible for the outcome of your life but the choices you make.

We all make active and passive choices daily, and the culmination of those choices is the ultimate determinant of the quality of our lives. Your present situation is a product of your past decisions, and your future depends on the choices you are making now. There is a need for individual accountability and a sense of responsibility in the way you make decisions. Anyone who fails to take full ownership of the outcome of his choice stands a chance of underutilizing the opportunities embedded in life's season. You cannot allow anyone to decide and design your life for you, because at the end of the day, you will be the ultimate beneficiary of whatever you allow in your life. You cannot afford to submit to fate by saying, "*Que sera sera*," whatever will be will be. Actually, what you allow will be allowed, and what you disallow will be disallowed.

Destiny is a matter of choice, not a matter of chance. It is not something to be waited for; it is something to be lived out. Living out your life will require a focused and deliberate effort on your part. You are the sole custodian of your destiny. Blaming others for your woes will not solve your problems but will instead compound them. If, for whatever reason, you are not okay with the life you are living now, you can choose to redesign your life and pay the price required to live the life you desire. Every choice has a price tag attached to it. What is the cost of your choice? Until you get to a point in your life where you are willing to dare and face difficult situations and seasons squarely, you may not be able to access the blessings in your seasons.

> *The success you have not achieved is the choice you have not made.*

When Abraham Lincoln chose to succeed politically, multiple failed attempts could not discourage him from the pursuit of his dreams. When you grasp the understanding of the concept of choice in life and you determine to design the kind of life you desire, none of life's seasons will be unproductive for you, no matter how difficult and challenging things may appear.

Not making a choice is a choice in itself. Making the right decision in life depends on your ability to know what you want in life. Never treat your life like a casino.

When you gamble with life, you will fumble in life.

Playing blame game can never excuse you from the consequences of your choice. Don't base your life on other people's opinion. One of the cheapest commodities in life is opinion. It is available in abundance, so much so that everyone has an idea about how you ought to live your life. Even in marital relationships, you cannot blame your spouse for your woes. I would have excused Adam from the influence of Eve in eating the forbidden fruit; however, he had a choice to decide not to eat the fruit despite the pressure from his wife. His excuse to God could not excuse him away from the consequences of his decision.

Abigail's story in the book of 1 Samuel 25 is an excellent example of personal accountability. She was a woman married to a complicated man and had a choice to be a bully like him, but instead, she chose to be generous. Her refusal to be influenced by the husband's negative behavior saved her household from destruction, when David decided to massacre every male in the family because of the husband's behavior. She successfully overturned a death sentence from an angry and desperate warrior.

The choices you make will eventually make you and can either keep you in time or behind time.

There is nothing in life that cannot be changed if you are willing to make a choice not to leave things up to chance.

I must emphasize that making a choice especially in the midst of multiple options can be very complicated and overwhelming. Life, as it were, will never present one option to you. You will face a never-ending task of choosing between multiple options. Your pick will determine your opportunity cost, and unfortunately, many people have made their original purpose the opportunity cost in life.

Have you ever thought of the reason a man would opt to take his life? Your purpose will always give you a reason to exist. If you can find your passion, it will not be difficult to discover your purpose.

One major prerequisite to making a good and purposeful choice in life lies in the discovery of who you are—your uniqueness. My book, 'The Problem of Identity" has resources that can help you resolve identity issues. Until you come to terms with who you are created to be and accept your uniqueness, you stand the chance of living a confused life.

CHAPTER 3

YOU ARE UNIQUE!

When you allow men to determine your worth, they will cheapen your value.

Have you ever wondered why your fingerprints are unique, such that no other person in the whole world can duplicate the print? Even the fingerprints of identical twins differ. We may try to explain this scientifically, but the mystery behind this remains that God did not create any two people to be the same. There is something about you that is unique beyond your gender, the color of your skin, or your height. The day you discover your uniqueness and show up, you will automatically become a pacesetter. You are uniquely fashioned and wired with a distinct purpose! No one has ever been created, or will be created, like you. You are a masterpiece, uniquely framed and wired with distinctive talents and features.

Until you accept your uniqueness, no one else will. What you call yourself is what people will call you. It does not matter what haters choose to call you. As long as you don't answer to it, it can never impact you. Moses claimed he was the meekest man who ever lived and that is what we all believed years after his demise. John wrote about being Jesus's favorite and being especially loved by Him among all others, and we agree with what he wrote and often call him John the Beloved. Mohammed Ali called himself the greatest, and people readily agreed with him.

How do you see yourself? What do you say about yourself? Here is what I say about myself: I am an amazing black woman, fearfully and wonderfully made. I'm bold, beautiful, smart, elegant, strong, fearless, responsible, innovative, hardworking, strategic, powerful, creative, confident, wise, adventurous, blessed, favored, unstoppable, industrious, prosperous, great, kind, generous, prayerful, appreciative, excellent, optimistic, determined, talented, resilient, tough, hopeful, tenacious, purposeful, and *unique*—a complete package of God's goodness and grace! I am what I am, and that's what nobody else can ever be.

Whatever word you put after *I am* will always form your reality. You may not be perfect, and probably will never be on this terrestrial; however, you need to stop focusing on your imperfections and start embracing your strengths, your uniqueness, and accept *you*.

Never think everybody will approve of you, and never allow anybody to put you down. The moment you come to terms with your uniqueness and choose to show up and live your dreams, you will automatically face opposition from people who are still confused about who they are.

> *A man who has discovered his uniqueness is never threatened or intimidated by other people's dreams or achievements.*

You need to start gravitating toward people who will lift you and add value to your life instead of hanging out with people who will put you down and make you feel worthless. A young boy once asked his father the value of his life. To teach the boy a life lesson, the father decided to engage the boy on a task that will profoundly answer the question. He gave the boy a small stone and asked him to sell it at the market with a unique instruction: When asked how much you want to sell it for, raise two fingers without speaking a word.

The boy went to the market, and, sure enough, he met a potential buyer who asked him the price of the stone. When he raised two fingers as instructed, the person said, "You mean two dollars?"

The lad went home and told the father that he got a buyer who valued the stone at two dollars. The man then told the son, "Take the stone to the museum and do the same thing you did at the market when asked for the price." When the boy got to the museum, he met a man who asked him the price of the stone. He raised two fingers without saying a word. The man looked at the boy and said, "Two hundred dollars?"

The boy did not respond. He went home and reported back to the father with excitement. "I met a man who was willing to pay two hundred dollars for the stone!"

The father then told him, "I need you to take the stone to one last place, the precious stone store, and do the same thing you did at the market and museum when asked for the price."

When the boy showed the stone to the store owner, the man was excited and exclaimed, "This is a rare gem!' How much do you want to sell it for?"

The boy raised two fingers, and the precious stone store owner said, "Two hundred thousand dollars? I will buy it."

The boy got confused and ran speedily home to his father. He told the father, "I can't believe the store owner wants to pay two hundred thousand dollars for this stone. I could have sold it for two dollars."

Then the father said to his son, "I can tell you the value of your life now. Your positioning will determine your worth. You can choose to place yourself in the market for two dollars or the museum for two hundred dollars or the precious stone store for two hundred thousand dollars. It all depends on you. When you allow people to determine your worth based on their understanding or perspective, they can reduce you to nothing."

The beginning of frustration in life is rooted in comparing yourself to others or trying to be who people think you should be. Do not let anyone define who you are or who you ought to be. Your first adventure before the quest to understand life and its seasons is to discover yourself and accept who you are. You can never become someone else, no matter how hard you try.

The best of another person you can be is an imitation.

I am yet to find two originals of the same thing; your value lies in your originality. Imitation is always lesser in value than the original.

You can never be good enough for people who are ignorant, jealous, confused, and lacking in personal direction. You can never be good enough for people who do not know your purpose, your capacity and capabilities, your journey, and your experience. You will not be good enough for people who do not know your pain and struggles, your fears, and the obstacles you have to deal with in life. You will not be good enough for people who see your strength as aggression. You will not be good enough for people who look at your confidence as arrogance. You will not be good enough for people who see your dream as a threat and your success as intimidation. You will not be good enough for people who have chosen not to see anything good about you—and these people, sincerely, have no relevance to your fulfillment in life. There will always be people who think you are less than who you are or trying to become.

I remember when Barack Obama first made his intention known to run for the presidency in the United States. Many millions of people across the globe saw his aspiration as an implausible idea. He was no match to his very first competition based on experience, influence, affluence, and pedigree. Nobody knew him. His last name sounded funny and weird to many. Despite the opposing view I have regarding some of his political agenda and policies, he is one of the very few people in the political arena I respect and applaud for his audacity. It goes down in history that one man dared to believe in himself and became the trailblazer for others like him who will dare to dream and venture into an unknown realm and an unfamiliar path.

Recount the story of David, a renowned political leader of Israel. His brother saw his confidence and convictions in challenging Goliath as arrogance because they did not have a clue about his experience in the desert. Their conclusion about David's destiny was that it was limited to sheep-shearing and running errands. They did not know that he was a trained warrior who victoriously fought beastly animals. They assumed the qualification for fighting Goliath was enrollment in the army of Saul, and if you were not part of the military, you didn't belong. David knew who he was and could not be convinced otherwise.

Never allow people who are clueless about your journey talk you out of your convictions. You must be willing to stand alone. When you allow men to determine your worth, they will cheapen your value. You are worth more than you think!

Knowing and accepting your uniqueness is critical to understanding the seasons of your life. One of the gateways to a frustrated life is the desire to compare your life experience with others or try to compete with people around you. The only competition you should have in life is with yourself. I have chosen not to be the best in my life because there is something better than best. Being best is subject to other people's performance. If you score highest in an exam at 50 percent, you are automatically the best among underperformers, even though there is a possibility of scoring 100 percent. I prefer "excellent" over "best."

Best is the enemy of excellence.

You need to compete with the person you have imagined yourself to become. Take time to discover and meet with the real you. You and you alone can reveal your talents and natural endowments. It is a disconcerting fact that many died, and many more are dying, without getting to meet who they are.

Until you discover yourself, nobody can find you. I urge you to embark on a quest to self-discovery. Do all you can, regardless of your experience, to know yourself before you die. There is so much about you that you need to know.

I did not discover the writer in me until 2012. When I had the inclination to write my first book on leadership, the first person I told about that dream looked at me straight in the eye and said, "You cannot write a book. It is impossible. How do you want to do it?"

Sincerely, that utterance was what provoked the dormant writer in me. Despite my very tight schedule, I made up time to write my very first book, and I discovered then that the book was within me. I only needed to look inward and deliver what I already conceived. The fact that people around you cannot acknowledge that you have the potential for greatness cannot deny or delay your delivery. You have the power to stand against the forces of abortion around you, which often present through spoken words. People will often offer you advice or ideas and speak words that can kill your vision and abort your dream. You must find courage enough to face the opposition, which usually comes from close acquaintances and families. Never accept an alternative for your uniqueness. Don't change who you are because you want to fit in.

> *Negotiations are vital in life, but never make negotiations with foolishness.*

People who are destined to be part of your life are going to gravitate to you based on your uniqueness. An eagle trying to peck around like chicken can never soar. The natural habitat for a fish is water. The day it decides to live on a tree like a bird is the day it will begin to die. The destiny and leadership of the lion are in the jungle; any attempt to fly will only bring ridicule and shame. As long as it remains in the wild, he will always roar and dominate with ease. Your uniqueness has a connection with your ideas, dreams, vision, and competencies. You can never function efficiently and productively outside your natural abilities. Your quest to be like someone else is a reflection of the emptiness within you.

If you glimpse into the private life of the individual you are desperately trying to be like, you will think twice. Not aspiring to be like someone else is not to underplay the importance of having a mentor, which is critical to understanding life's seasons. However, your quest for mentoring should be to receive guidance and acquire knowledge, not to be like your mentor.

> *Strive to learn from others, but never aspire to be like any.*

Also, being unique does not make you superior to other people around you. You are in no way better than another person. If the people you feel superior to have the same privileges you had, they might have come out better than you, and if you had to walk in the shoes of some of the people you look down on, your life probably might have been worse than theirs. It is essential to understand the importance of staying humble in life. Please know that the people you look down on today may turn out to become the people you will look up to tomorrow.

Embracing your uniqueness demands that you surround yourself with people you can collaborate or synergies with, those who have strength in your areas of weaknesses and vulnerabilities. There will be moments in life that you will need others. You cannot live in isolation. Creation echoes the need for interdependent relationship. The ecosystem makes it very clear that nothing is created for itself. You are never designed to live to and for yourself. Your interpersonal relationship skills have a lot to do in determining the quality of your life. You need to surround your life with great minds, people who can enhance your life and also look for people you too can bless. Your uniqueness ought to make you simultaneously a protégé and a mentor. Life becomes dead when you live in isolation. The Dead Sea is dead because it only takes but does not give out. No wonder it has no life. Many lives lack fulfillment and meaning because they are closed up.

I am naturally shy and was never someone who would initiate a conversation. However, over the years, I have come to realize that an introvert is deficient in many ways. When you fail to speak up, you go through your pain and struggles alone. Often, you are prone to making a wrong decision during moments of deep life crisis, which is inevitable. You do not necessarily have to become a social bee. However, it is vital that you move out of your comfort zone and learn to speak up and reach out as much as you can. In your uniqueness, you must be open to growth. Never stay rigid and continue to be who you used to be. It is essential for you to be willing to adjust your lifestyle to your situation or needs in a positive way, without compromising principles and values.

The Mindset

It is practically impossible for me to talk about understanding life and its seasons without providing an insight into the mind. The mind, as it were, is the origin of life's actions and inactions. The most significant investment you can ever make in life is never in real estate or stocks or other forms of financial and tangible investments. The most rewarding and worthwhile investment any person can make is in his mind. Everything in life and about life stems from it. The mind is the foundation and fountain for either success or failure. You will always be a product of your mindset. No one can embrace his uniqueness without dealing with the issues of his mind. Your mind is the incubator of your life choices and actions. It can be your greatest assets as well as your greatest liability, depending on how skilled you are at engaging your mind. Nothing in life can overcome you until your mind is defeated. Until you change your mindset, you can never change your life and embrace your uniqueness. Your mindset can make you see problems as opportunities or opportunities as problems.

> *What you conceive in your mind will determine what you will deliver in life.*

Until your mind receives liberation, your life can never experience freedom. A mediocre mind can never live an extraordinary life. The mind is so powerful that it influences your choices, desire, and lifestyle, quietly and subtly, based on the environment you are exposed to on your life path. Your mind can be conditioned for either failure or success and will attract to your life whatever has been programmed into it, even in the face of opportunities. Many slaves opted to remain enslaved to their masters after they were declared emancipated because it was practically impossible for them to wrap their mind around a life of freedom. They had been conditioned to a life of servitude, and they adopted and adapted to that lifestyle and were not willing to adjust to a life outside slavery.

Every life's battle targets the mind. You lose your mind when it can no longer handle the inevitable pressures of life.

Every life experience will have its dose of life's challenges. However, it will always come in different and unique packages. It is imperative to prepare your mind and empower yourself for life's highs and lows.

The computer is the most common equipment I can compare to the mind. Whatever you input in your mind, consciously or consciously, will determine your life's output, just like the old computer slogan: "Garbage in, garbage out." The autocorrect feature in many people's mind is so active, because of what they have stored in their subconscious mind, that it is difficult to write new things. It is constantly bringing suggestions based on memories. One thing is very certain in life: As we grow older, we accumulate memories, pleasant and otherwise. All the numerous experiences over time forms beliefs and opinions that set the mind in certain ways. Making new decisions based solely on suggestions from a mindset of hurt, disappointment, failure, and mediocrity can only deliver the same old results. To embrace a new thing, you must do things differently. Many minds require formatting or pushing the "delete" button. The question is how do you format your mind? How do you break away from old habits? How do you change your deficient thinking patterns? How do you equip your mind always to see the good in every situation? The truth is there is always going to be a positive outcome in every adversity. It depends on your "life's processor"—the mind. You may need a whole new processor to move to the next level. Changing or updating the mind can only happen when you embrace intentional living. I want to recommend the book, "The Power of Habit" by Charles Duhigg if you need further help in breaking old habits and developing new ones.

To engage your mind, you must be able to guard and guide your senses appropriately. Humans' senses play a significant role in determining the state of his mind. What you hear, what you see, and what you perceive over time will form the realities in your mind. At times, you may need to change your environment, not necessarily your location but mostly your association—people and things that speak to your life. Your choice of music and movie genres, the types of books you read and, your leisure activities.

I heard the story of a young elephant who was tied to a tree at a very early age and could only move in circles within the length of the rope that was used to tie him down. With time, the elephant has developed the strength to pull the weight of limitations down and be free. Unfortunately, over the years, his mind has been conditioned to walking in circles, and that was all it continued to do, despite its potential strength, which it could engage anytime to liberate itself. Many people are the same as that elephant. Despite the potential they have for excellence, their life experiences over the years have put them inside a mental cage so that the only thing they can see and respond to are limitations. The worst prison anyone can be locked in is the prison of his mind.

Another analogy that comes to mind is Pavlov's experiment on conditioning. Many minds have been conditioned to respond only to specific stimulus, and without that familiar stimulus, they remain stagnant. Regardless of what was packaged in your mind—failure or limitations—you can unlearn any learned behavior if you are intentional about life.

Updating and resetting the mind is so unique that it cannot be a one-size-fits-all remedy. It all depends on where you have been in life, where you are now, what you are dealing with, and how much investment you are willing to make in your mind.

The state of your mind will determine how you handle the seasons of life. Your will power is a function of your mindset. Before you proceed to the subsequent chapters in this book, I want you to take time and do a self-reflection on your mindset, most importantly, your subconscious mind, which is the reservoir of diverse life experiences. The subconscious mind is your resource for handling life situation based on what it has been fed overtime. If you have any unresolved issue in your past, you have the tendency of failing in that aspect of your life when faced with similar situation. Paul, a renowned Roman and Jewish author, wrote about the importance of daily renewal of mind which is the path to transformation (Romans 12:2). I want to recommend the book, "The Hidden Man" by E.W. Kenyon or "The Battlefield of the Mind" by Joyce Meyer if you need further help in dealing with the issues of the mind.

Life seasons are in cycles and your experience of success or failure can hinder or limit your future progress until you make an intentional and conscious effort to break the cycle.

Take a retrospective look into your life experiences before the age of 21.

1. List all your disappointments and failures that you were unable to resolve.
2. Identify the barriers that prevented you from getting the issues resolved.
3. Come up with a strategic resolution plan on how to resolve similar issues in the future.
4. List five limitations you have faced in life

5. Identify people who are doing well in areas where you are limited
6. Make intentional connections with them to provide mentoring and resource that can help you overcome your barriers
7. List significant "successful" experience in your life
8. Are there people who outperform you in areas of your recorded success?
9. Meet with them to learn what they did differently
10. Develop a daily routine on how to engage your conscious mind on things that can enhance your life
11. Replace bad habits with new ones
12. Be intentional about your thought process

Activities 7 to 9 are important because there is always room for improvement. If your mind is conditioned on past experience of success, you have the tendency of taking things for granted and lose when the game changes. There is always a new and better way of doing things and winning in life.

As we transition to the different life's season's, please keep this in mind:

Summing it all up, friends, I'd say you'll do best by filling your minds and meditating on things true, noble, reputable, authentic, compelling, gracious—the best, not the worst; the beautiful, not the ugly; things to praise, not things to curse. Put into practice what you learned from me, what you heard and saw and realized. Do that, and God, who makes everything work together, will work you into his most excellent harmonies - Philippians 4:8-9 MSG

CHAPTER 4

SEASONS OF PREPARATION

Ignorance and indecision will always put you at a disadvantage when life's opportunities come your way.

Nothing don't just happen!

You will always be responsible for the happenings in your life regardless of your passivity and indifference. You might not have been instrumental to the decision that brought you to life; however, you are ultimately responsible for the quality of the life you will live. I love to read autobiographies, and this has helped me to know that while your upbringing can present limitations in life, you cannot be limited until you accept the limitations. LeBron James's mother had him at sixteen to a father with a criminal history, yet he made it through the pursuit of his purpose. James Robinson was a product of rape and was given up for adoption. The circumstances surrounding his birth could not limit him in life.

You are not the only one with limitations; every human has some form of hindrance. Your decision over time will determine the outcome of your life. Planning your life with intention is vital to your ability to take control of life's circumstances, understanding life complexities and its seasons. There is a common saying: He who fails to plan plans to fail. Unfortunately, many people are negligent in preparation or probably ignorant of the importance of preparing for life. As I grow older and gain a better perspective on life, I have come to realize that most of the deficient aspects of my life were in areas I had failed to prepare for adequately or took for granted, while my areas of recorded success were those I approached with adequate preparation and focused intention. You may know what you want in life, but if you are not prepared to give it whatever it will take, you may end up in the land of compromise, since there are people and situations along life's path who will try to convince you out of your convictions or make you doubt your strengths, talents, and abilities.

One of the most tragic things in life is for someone to be confused about what they want. I have seen people go to college and have no sense of direction regarding their future. Their major is "undecided," and they keep changing until change eventually change them by handing them leftovers. I had the chance to interview a young graduate who applied for a patient-care technician position. After reviewing her resume, my passion for helping people find their hidden path in life became more intense. She graduated cum laude from an accredited four years college in the United States and continued to work as a cashier at a fast food restaurant. Sitting across the table from her, I had many questions going through my head. Why did she go to college? I wouldn't want to waste time going to college if my life would not be enhanced. Was her career goal clearly defined? Did she take advantage of the career services on campus? Does she have a mentor or a life coach? Had she discovered her worth? I saw in her lots of potential, but it was caged inside confusion. She needs a guiding light. I couldn't give her the PCT job, but I gave her something more—insight into her world that is full of possibilities. I was successful in taking hold of the switch to her mind and turning on the light. At the end of our meeting, she decided to go back to school for a bridge program that would help her build a career path. The last time she called me, she had already decided the school she was going to attend and was scheduled to start the next semester.

Ignorance and indecision will always put you at a disadvantage when life's opportunities come your way. Every single day of your life and every path you take in life presents tons of opportunities that are only available to a prepared mind. There is no such things as good luck when you have failed to prepare adequately to take advantage of life opportunities or combat life's adversities as they come through your path. The only family that was preserved during the first flood recorded in human history prepared before the rain started. If they did not put things in place through hard work and focus on building the ship, there would have been no place of refuge for the people who escaped the destruction from the flood.

Preparation is hard work and should be a priority in your life. You need to invest more time, energy, and resources in preparing than anything else.

Indecision is an enemy of preparation in life.

You can never arrive at a future you have not envisioned.

It is critical for you to sit down and decide what you want from life and in life. As soon as you can grasp the idea of what you desire your life output to be, you must be deliberate and intentional in putting plans in place toward accomplishing your goals. Dreams without a plan are futile, and actions without a plan are fatal. Many have become a casualty of their deeds due to failure to prepare adequately before launching out on life's adventure. Any structure of worth is, first of all, envisioned before manifestation. The little I know about architectural engineering makes the issue of planning and preparation critical to a well-structured life. No builder can start construction on any building until the design of the house is completed and approved. The government enforces the building regulation and outlines consequences for violations, since any unplanned structure carries the potential for a fatal hazard. Code violations have warranted the need to demolish buildings that pose a threat to safety. If we are so meticulous about planning a building that is of limited worth, I think having a plan for the structure and the design of our lives should be more critical. The disorderliness and chaos we see daily in our society stems from an unstructured life. When you build your life on a faulty foundation, the structure will collapse over time.

Some time ago, we wanted to buy a house, and we were excited because of the price; it was a steal! We went for the appraisal and inspection, and I was curious to know why the house was so cheap. The expert, who had in-depth knowledge in building, pointed to a crack on the wall. He then said, "It was cheap because the house has a problem with the foundation." By the time he outlined the potential cost of repair, I did not need any conviction to stop the pursuit of purchasing that particular property. A life that is not well planned at the foundational level can be very costly to repair. Part of the reason why change seems unrealistic for many is due to foundational problems and the enormity of the sacrifice required to making the changes.

You always have access to everything you need to lead a fulfilled life, as long as you know what you want and you are willing to give it what it will take. It may not be easy, but it's not impossible. It is also crucial to understand that it will take a process for you to arrive at the future you have envisioned. I was able to engage an architect in a conversation regarding building design, and this is what he had to say: "It takes a process. Your ability to see the final layout before construction allows for the opportunity to make changes and move things around without hassles. It is costly and overwhelming to make changes to an already finished building, especially if the issue is with the foundation. The floor plan provides guidance on where to swing the hammer, pull down a wall, create a doorway, and help reduce error." I was involved in the planning of a building project and everything had to be delayed because the city was not going to grant the permit until all the building codes requirements were satisfied. One of the requirements is a plan for emergency exit. What is the escape route if there is a fire outbreak, where is the safe zone for tornado and storms?

Do you have a life plan? How prepared are you for emergencies? The most devastating life events are often the ones without a prior plan for eventualities. I remember September 11, 2011 incident in the United States. I was in one of the elementary schools working as a substitute teacher when the tragic news was announced. Almost everybody agreed that a lack of preparedness made the situation worse. The airport security plan was not designed with an attack of that magnitude in mind. Everyone was caught unaware. Things do happen; however, adequate preparation can help minimize negative impact.

> *"The man who is prepared, has his battle half fought"*
> *- Miguel De Cervantes*

Often, we make decisions based on where we are and not where we are going. This book is not focused on the subject of purpose and vision; however, you need to understand the two concepts for adequate preparation for life. When the two are not clearly defined you have the tendency of getting confused. If you need help in defining your life's vision, my book on leadership has insightful information that can provide guidance. I will also recommend Dr. Myles Munroe's book on "Purpose"

Choosing a spouse is one critical area where most people lack adequate preparation. I am in no way perfect in this area; however, life events have taught me the importance of planning for life. When you choose a man or woman based on your *now*, without factoring in your eventual destination in life, you stand the chance of dealing with a crisis, mainly if one of the partners evolves and discovers purpose on a different path later in the relationship. Always remember that the man or woman you are trying to hook up with already has a foundation you cannot change; you can only build on that foundation. Unfortunately, in the same way you cannot see the foundation of any building on the surface, there is always a depth to every individual hidden from you. The only way you can make a change is to destroy the foundation and start over. It is easier to reconstruct and remodel a building but very daunting to rebuild the foundation of any building—you cannot change anyone but you!

I am currently working on a book, *The Complexities of Marriage*, based on my life experience and that of others whose private lives I have been privileged to glimpse into. I have sat in conferences and seminars held by acclaimed marriage experts, and sometimes I am bewildered by the same rhetoric on love, sex, and finance in sustaining a marriage. More than that is needed for the sustainability of any marital relationship, and it's always going to be unique, based on the peculiarity and the foundational values, principles, and upbringing of the couples. The interesting thing is that most deep relationship issues are difficult to articulate because of shame and regret. Often, before marriage, you only get to meet one person out of probably seven or more personalities living in the same body. What do you do when you discover the other hidden characters? The furious person that shows up once in a decade but can destroy everything in the twinkling of an eye. How about the lazy person, or the selfish and promiscuous one? We bring children to life without adequate preparation to help them have a decent living. You don't have to be rich to create decency for your children. The underpinnings of any life preparation that works are on principles and values. When parents lack values and principles that govern their actions in life, this lack of values will ultimately impact the children now or later. It breaks my heart when I see children brought into the world to raise themselves or allow to go through suffering. I think it is the highest form of cruelty and disservice to humanity to make innocent kids go through rigor and hardship because of the lack of preparation for life on the part of the parents. We have access to genetic testing, and yet we take a chance on life and allow children to live with illnesses. Yes, I do understand there are things we cannot control, and I was very explicit on the concept of choice earlier. For instance, we would not be having any more issues with sickle cell disease if parents were intentional about life. We cannot blame the government for the degeneration in our society. It starts from you and me. To fix the community, we need to address individual problems.

There was a dad who was being disturbed by his four-year-old son. In an attempt to keep the boy busy, he gave him a task to assemble pieces of world puzzle. In his mind, the activity will help him get two hours of focus on his work. He was amazed when the boy came back with the completed puzzle in about ten minutes. Out of curiosity, he asked the boy how he was able to put all the countries and locations together so fast. The boy took the puzzle from the father and turned it over. On the back was the picture of a man. He said to the father, "All I did was put the body parts in place. When I put the man together, I put the world together." To fix our society, we need to address individual issues. A planned life will impact a planned family, a planned family will influence a planned community, and a planned community will yield a planned nation.

The season of preparation in life is perpetual and also the most vital of any life. It does not matter the season you are in; you will always need to prepare for the next season, which inevitably will evolve, whether you are ready for it or not. Every season is bound to change, for better or worse.

Nothing good lasts forever, and nothing bad lasts forever.

Preparation for life and in life is broad and unique for every individual. You will agree with me that most of the areas of your life that you devoted ample time to prepare for often come out with a positive result and outlook with no surprises. Even when things didn't go as planned, you have an understanding of the reasons for failure or setbacks, and you are prepared to take a detour as needed without compromising your purpose. If you set out of your house with a specific destination in mind, no roadblock can prevent you from getting to your destination. The worst that can happen will be for you to take a detour, since you already know where you are going, and you are fully prepared to get there. Failure in life is never a hindrance to a prepared mind. When plan A fails, you can always use the same strategy to come up with a plan B.

Preparation in life helps you identify your strengths, weaknesses, and limitations. It also enables you to earnest your resources appropriately. If you plan on building a three-story building, preparation helps you face the reality of your capacity in completing it. If all you have is only enough for a two-bedroom bungalow, you can make a sound decision and redirect your plans based on your reality or source for more funds to help in implementing your project. If you did not prepare well before implementation, you are bound to face frustrations and regrets, and that is absolutely the story of many lives. I tried to engage someone in a conversation about a project he was attempting to implement, and I was sincerely scared about his thought process. It was difficult to wrap my mind around his thinking patterns. My question was how can you implement a project without adequate planning? There was no due diligence, no feasibility studies or market mapping whatsoever. Success in life may not be easy, but it is predictable, based on the effectiveness or ineffectiveness of planning. Never base your life on assumptions. The next time you have a crisis in your life or things get out of control, you must sit back and ask yourself the question, "Is this a planning issue?" If you don't identify your deficiencies in this area, you will continue to make the same mistake, frustrating yourself and the people around you. There is no substitute for planning. You need to engage your sense, and God has given everyone a measure of reasoning, and, sincerely, if you are deficient in an area, you can glean wisdom from people with better intelligence in that area. I don't have all the answers, but I do know how to identify people who have what it takes to accomplish an excellent outcome in specific areas of life where I am deficient. You are better off letting people know you don't know. However, you can turn yourself to an object of ridicule when you act as if you know but you are ignorant.

Life comes with gains and pain.

> *Adequate preparation will help you see the gain in life adversities in spite of the pain.*

Many people who claimed to prepare for life only look forward to the gains and not the pain. A matured mind understands the need to anticipate and put measures in place to deal with inevitable life tragedies—it is part of the package! How do you handle pain and disappointment when it comes knocking your door? Failure to prepare adequately for life's eventualities is a gateway to depression, hatred, the blame game, and suicide in some cases. Pain will come in different forms: the pain of rejection, betrayal, setbacks, unreciprocated love, and loss of business, disappointments, failed health—sincerely, the list is endless. Take a moment and write out some of the "what ifs?" of life that you have not yet imagined—those unpleasant life realities that you dread and cannot envisage happening to your worst enemy. What if they happen to you? How will you handle them? Life is full of contradictions!

I will talk more on "seasons of contradiction" in a later chapter. However, failure to prepare for life's contradictions can weigh you down or take you out if you are not prepared. Life is never a fantasy; it is real! Adequate preparation helps you to be strategic in life. It helps you identify potential pitfalls, to avoid them, and to put measures in place to control impending damages if they are unavoidable.

Many people across the globe could not wrap their mind around how Donald Trump was able to emerge as the President of the United States despite his many flaws, his lack of "relevant" credentials in the political arena, and his deficient public-speaking skills (based on the standards set by his predecessors). One thing that is unique about him that earned him the victory lies in his adequate preparation. I followed his story and the interview he had in 1988 with Oprah Winfrey. It was effortless to reconcile the discrepancy between what most people thought before he won and the reality after he won. He envisioned the route to the White House way before he embarked on the journey. He knew who and what he was going to compete with and understood the need to become a standard in his class instead of joining the existing standards.

Sometimes, you may need to create your path especially if you don't fit in with status quo. Your inability to fit in with the cliques is a pointer that you need to create your path and be a trailblazer. Trump was very strategic and intentional about winning. He understood he could not win on the Democratic platform but could penetrate the Republican Party based on the loopholes he identified in the party. He also used what he had to get what he wanted. He did not need any financial assistance or sponsorship from anyone for his campaign. He knew the type of audience that would listen to him and agree with his barbaric ideology. He literally redefined American politics and made many question the integrity of our values and principles— especially when it comes to bullying. The fact is you don't need to like or agree with him, but you can learn from him. Learn to identify your limitations and strengths, your resources, your opposition, life opportunities, and the type of people you need around you to win in life and make preparations to win at your game before you launch out. Preparation is what helps you take advantage of life's opportunities when they come your way. And yes, there are abundant opportunities on life's path.

> *Adequate preparation makes you a standard and a pacesetter in life.*

Recently, I was watching an interview on the preparation around the movie *Black Panther,* which took four years of groundwork before it was released, and I was not surprised when one of the cast stated that the very first task they embarked on was to prepare. A four-week boot camp to address their general physique was needed for the movie, as well as an individual physical training based on each cast member's role.

The story that readily came to mind when I was watching the interview was the first beauty pageant recorded in human history. All the participants were required to prepare for a whole year before they could get a chance to appear before the king and have the opportunity to be considered for the palace. Gaining access to the platform you desire in life will require intentional preparation. I have had people talk about favor factor, and realistically, favor does not work in isolation. It is only for a prepared mind. Praying for a favor to get a job you do not qualify for is like building a castle in the air. Favor did not work for Esther, the winner of the beauty contest, without adequate preparation. She had seven beauticians working on her physique for twelve months. She sought advice from the person coordinating the competition on strategies for winning and followed the instructions and guidelines suggested to her.

Never appear on life platforms without preparation because there are specific platforms you can only get once in a lifetime and when you miss it, you miss destiny. I was scheduled to interview someone for a job position, and sincerely, my jaw opened when the person showed up in a tracksuit and was making excuses about his appearance. Of course, I was very polite and carried out the interview, although briefly, for formality's sake. However, before the interview, I had made up my mind not to offer him the job. I was looking for more than his skills and resume. I saw a disorganized, carefree, laid-back individual that did not have the personality I was looking for, even though his resume looked perfect. A lesson I have learned in managing people is that I can teach the skills to get the job done; however, I cannot change anyone's personality, and every job requires specific personality for effectiveness. How do you appear on life's stage? Your appearance will determine what you attract and whether people will buy into what you have to offer.

> *Adequate preparation gives you a chance and a platform in life.*

The people you surround yourself with can either enhance your preparedness for life or endanger it. Solomon, a famous king in Israel and the acclaimed wisest man who ever lived, had a mother who helped him prepare for a future that seemed impossible. Based on birthrights ordinance and Eastern culture, the first son is the heir apparent. Here is a guy whose mother cheated on her former husband and got him killed. The history was not a pleasant one; however; Solomon's mother was a strategic planner. She targeted the throne for her son and built the right kind of relationship needed for the young man to make it, despite the odds against him. He survived every opposition as a result of adequate planning. He was enshrined before he got to the throne. The heir apparent lost the throne to an opponent who adequately and strategically prepared for the throne. You stand a chance of losing what rightfully belongs to you if you lack preparedness skills. Survival is easier for the fittest. Do not take things for granted, since other people are willing to contest for things that are rightfully yours. Lack of preparation has led to the extinction of much potential. The person who ought to be the king took things for granted and did not prepare. He assumed his positioning based on the birth order was the only requirement for the throne. He failed to build the right relationships and have relevant conversations. He did not go through mentoring to acquire the skills needed for the position that potentially belonged to him and ended up a loser. The utilization of every potential requires preparation. Preparation precedes planting. A prudent farmer understands the importance of clearing and cultivating the ground before attempting to plant. Failure to prepare the soil before planting put the seed at survival risk in the face of thorns and thistles. Lack of preparedness put all your potential at risk for failure. You need to identify the right location for your dream.

Before planting your business idea in a location, it's crucial that you complete due diligence regarding the market. What is your potential competition? What are the threats to your survival? Do you have enough resources to overcome the opposition, or do you need reinforcement? Can you operate alone, or will you need to partner with people of like mind or others with complementary skills? Launching out without thorough due diligence and strategic planning can frustrate all your efforts. Planning is the roadmap to get to your future.

CHAPTER 5

SEASONS OF PLANTING

He who fails to plant, has no hope of harvest.

You have a seed to plant, no matter how impoverished and deficient you think you are. Your seed is what will earn you the desired harvest, and it is practically impossible for you to reap without sowing. A seed remains irrelevant and insignificant without planting. Locked up in every seed is a "potential" to become a plant, a tree, or a forest based on how, when, and where the planting occurred, its potential, cultivation, and amount of nurturing. Likewise, locked up in every person is the great "potential" to become anything and everything in life. Potential according to Merriam Webster is something that can develop or become actual. Your seed is all your potential. The same way a seed is irrelevant until it is planted, your potential remains irrelevant without cultivation, and this requires a lot of work and commitment. The timeline required for the cultivation of your potential may vary based on its uniqueness. Every seed requires different timelines for growth and harvesting based on the genetic make-up of the seed.

Your planting season is that time you put all efforts into developing or growing your seed. You have to cultivate your talents intentionally, in a way that will make them presentable and desirable. This season is endless and requires that you continue to plant ceaselessly. As long as you have your breath, you must engage in active planting. Otherwise, you will have nothing to harvest in the future.

The fact that you have planted today does not imply that you will not need to plant tomorrow. Every stage of your life will require different planting for your next season or stage of life. You can predict your future based on what you are doing now. Where you are today is a product of what you or people who have access to your life planted yesterday. Where you will be tomorrow depends on what you are planting today.

> Though I do not believe that a plant will spring up where no seed has been, I have great faith in a seed. Convince me that you have a seed there and I am prepared to expect wonders.
> —Henry David Thoreau

One crucial precursor to planting is an expectation. What do you expect from life? If you do not have any expectations, you may find it difficult to plant. I have been privileged to interact with different people, and it saddens me anytime I see untapped potentials in people, especially in areas that are not commonly explored by the majority. Most people prefer to glean and lean on others instead of planting their seed. Indeed, planting your seed is a risk, since many factors will determine the eventual yield. Investing in a business is a risk, and any venture you undertake is a taking of risk. However, not planting your seed is riskier, since your chances at harvesting are null.

> *Life is either a daring adventure or nothing at all.*
> —*Helen Keller*

If you do your due diligence very well during the season of preparation, planting season should be more comfortable for you since you have prepared to be better able to focus your energy and channel your resources toward your goal. The identification of the type of seed you have for planting is critical. There are universal seeds that every human possess equally: time and life. Planting your time and life may not yield immediate results; however, if you are strategic and intentional in where you are planting, you will reap according to the quality of your seed. Ideas are seeds to be planted. What vision do you have for your future? Where do you see yourself in three years, five years, ten years, or retirement? These questions can provide insight on strategies to planting your seed. Your answers to them should determine the type of activities that should occupy your time.

Your entire life is a culmination of your daily activities. Everything will add up eventually.

Planting your time on frivolities will yield futility.

You sabotage yourself and possible opportunities when you play it safe during your planting season. You need to go all out and give life all it will take during this season, based on your seed and your expected harvest. You must be willing to take a risk without fear of disappointment. You will be more disappointed by not attempting than by failing at the risk you take. There are fundamental things to consider during your planting season in life. The type of seed you have will determine the kind of soil and environment to plant. The uniqueness of every seed is a determinant of the elements needed for its germination. Some seeds naturally grow without a lot of external influence, while others require a proportionate amount of water, oxygen, and temperature. Some can only thrive in darkness, while others need exposure to the right amount of sunlight.

Nature teaches us so many lessons about life's processes and principles that make things happen and predictable. Considering the outlined requirements for a seed to germinate, there is a similarity in the way you ought to approach your planting season as well. The uniqueness of your talents or "seeds" and what that talent need for development should determine how you plant. Often, we attempt to plant like others, not considering the specific demands of the seed we carry, and thus we get frustrated when the yield is not what we expected. You can predict your yield based on how you plant your seed. There is the need to understand the seed and its potential before planting. The seed should determine the type of soil and climate and not vice versa. Some plants, like the palm trees, will only come out in tropical weather. Almond trees do not thrive in a wet environment. Regardless of the quality of your seed, it can be corrupted or remain dormant if the environmental factors are not favorable and the soil you are planting on is not fertile. Here are some questions you should ask yourself anytime you are planting:

1. What seed do you want to plant?
2. Do you have an understanding of the seed genetic make-up?
3. Do you need a guiding light or an expert to guide you through the process?
4. What type of soil do you plan on planting your seed?
5. Did you take time to make sure the choice of land is relevant and favorable to the kind of seed you have?
6. Is the weather around you favorable to growing your seed?
7. What are the odds against the germination of your seed?
8. How long do you have to wait to see a yield?
9. Do you have enough resources to nurture your seed until maturity?
10. Do you have a survival plan while you wait for the harvest?

Please ponder over these questions and answer them with all sincerity. This will help you plant strategically.

I have seen people planting the seeds of time and intellect attend college and pursue a degree that has no relevance to society. Who will buy your fruits when they are ready to pick? Supporters or customers are not generally attracted to the people they follow or patronize based on their personality but rather their performance. When I do performance review for my teams, objectively, the focus is always on the job performance rather than personality. I can't promote you to the next level because you are a good person. You will need to have what it takes to produce the results expected for the job role.

I remember telling one of my stellar teammates how I wished I could make her into a social worker. Her personality was a perfect fit for the role. However, she didn't have the required credentials. There are certain things you simply cannot do because of regulatory requirements. I have hired people who were subpar character-wise but had the credentials and the skills to get the job done. Unfortunately, I had to learn how to manage and contain the personalities because they have the fruits needed to deliver the required results. To be truly outstanding, you need an exceptional personality to go along with your credentials. People will gravitate toward you based on the fruits you have to serve and what they need in their life. Never assume followership to be the same as friendship. Many famous people are lonely in the midst of the crowd. People don't care much about the person the way they care about the performance. You may be falling apart, but as long as you continue to deliver your fruits as expected, you can be sure of applause. Your relevance to the world is all about meeting a need.

Some seeds produce lifetime yield once planted; however, they take a long time to produce any yield. There are some that only produce once in a season and require ongoing planting for ongoing harvest. When the founder of Kentucky Fried Chicken (KFC) decided to plant the seed of his fried chicken recipe, he did not know that the seed he was planting would germinate into a legacy that would outlive him. Martin Luther King Jr. dared to plant his dream, a dream that seemed impossible. The dream pushed him to the edge of the cliff and gave him the option to fall or fail. Failing to plant his seed was not an option, and so he opted for falling as a symbol of planting. He knew his life was a seed, a seed to break the barriers of limitation, and until it fell to the ground, it could not die. The death of a seed is the gateway to a new life, a life containing more than what was planted. I want to assume that he was not the only one who had a vision of a nation where apparent segregation would become history. However, he was a prominent man who rallied others to buy into his dream. That singular act to pursue his dream, made him an icon to be remembered worldwide.

The very first global economic crisis reported in human history was resolved by a young man who chose to plant his seed despite opposition and adversity. This guy, Joseph, had a seed his family members despised. His ability to dream and interpret dreams was a prominent seed he had. His identification of that gift as a seed to be planted, and his determination to plant regardless of what others thought, landed him a job as the first economic adviser and prime minister of the world power of his time. By using his gift, providing strategic planning advice to the president of the most powerful nation of his generation, he saved the whole world from economic meltdown and social decay. He did not allow adversity to prevent him from planting his seed. He used the odds against him to his advantage. The development of his seed gained him much recognition, to the point that when a need arose that required the expertise of talents, he had no competition. The area of your dominion is limited to the type of talent you possess and your ability to develop and master your gifting.

LeBron James has dominated the basketball court because he planted his seed. He took the time to practice and equip himself for success before appearing on the platform of opportunity.

In the world of golf, Tiger Woods' father discovered the seed in Tiger and planted it at the age of four. That seed received the nurturing required for its translation to a world-class demand that would yield bounties to Tiger.

A valuable lesson from Joseph's experience was his willingness to provide free service to the person who referred him to Pharaoh. At times, you may need to work for free to develop your gift. The more you voluntarily use your gift, the better you will get at the skills. You never know who will notice you while you do voluntary service and recommend you for something higher and better. I have had promotion on the job because I volunteered to help out in an area of need. The volunteer activities exposed some of my hidden potentials and provided an opportunity for me to advance.

There will always be haters and naysayers when you attempt to plant your seed; please plant anyway. Never allow anyone to talk you out of your dream. Your dream is a seed that you need for your next level, and most times, it will never make sense to people.

The same way it takes time for a seed to germinate. Naturally, it will take time for you to see the results of your effort. Don't be discouraged if the expected results are not forthcoming. Keep cultivating the skills needed for the expression of your dream. The same way a natural seed will have to face certain odds against its germination, you will also face opposition that may want to compete against the manifestation of your dream. Be aware of envious people around you. Weed negative people out of your path the same way you will weed out thorns that will not allow your seed to germinate.

Your seed requires incubation before it can evolve into something beautiful and tangible. Your primary responsibility is to plant and select the appropriate environment for the nurturing of your seed. The potential outcome of the yield of everything you plant is already within the seed. Each seed carries a unique genetic code and the ability to bring forth new life as long as the conditions around it remain favorable.

It is critical to understand the nature of the seed you are carrying and its potential as you decide the location where you will plant. Your potential should determine your location. When you try to streamline your talents to adjust to the environment, you may kill the seed of your destiny. You need to choose your association based on your seed. You already carry the potential for greatness, and there is no man without a seed to plant. Please make sure you identify your seed and plant it with the expectations of harvest in mind. Some seeds will never germinate unless they are in the right location. Where you have planted yourself may be the source of your failure.

Every seed requires a period of latency while it's working at growing, based on the available nutrients or resources. The period of incubation is a very delicate period and requires a lot of focused attention. Likewise, if not incubated under favorable conditions, an egg, which is very comparable to the seed, may not hatch. Incubating the eggs of your dream will require time, resources, energy, dedication, and compromise. In the not-so-distant past, before the advanced technological development of artificial incubators, the mother hen had to do so much, sitting on her eggs instinctively to generate the heat needed for the new life to hatch. The period of incubation requires a lot of compromises.

1. What are you willing to sacrifice to incubate on your dream? In the pursuit of your goal and the development

of your talent, strive to maintain a healthy balance. Never compromise things or relationships you cannot afford to lose. I have seen people compromise family time in the pursuit of their career and end up losing their children. I once read the story of a renowned preacher, Eli. His dedication to the pastoral work compromised his children's upbringing, and he ended up losing everything—the children and the ministry altogether. Make sure you find a healthy balance as you engage your talents.

2. What are the odds against the birthing of your idea?
3. Do you have the time to sit on the eggs of your vision until they are ready to be hatched?
4. How about the temperature? Is it regulated or unregulated? Is the environment safe?
5. What type of alliance or mentoring do you need to survive?

You have to be intentional about where you are attempting to plant your seed. A healthy seed cannot thrive where the soil is barren. Even if the ground is fertile, you can still experience barrenness or lack of productivity, since certain seeds can only germinate in specific soil and temperature. Despite adequate preparation, the dynamics of things may change along the line. Your season of planting whatever seed is in your heart requires a constant evaluation of your plan. You have to be flexible and be willing to make compromises that will favor your expected outcome. Many have been frustrated because of rigidity and lack of readiness for change Sometimes you may have to employ the experience and expertise of others, depending on your capacity. It is okay to start small; dreams often fail when people attempt to skip the ladder. The experience through the process are resources you will need for personal growth. Never try to jump the process required for the achievement of your dream. If you fail or fall, it will be difficult to trace the cause of your failure.

Earning a bachelor's degree in mathematics was a significant accomplishment in my life because of the many life lessons it taught me. Every class has a prerequisite, and if you lack the understanding of the elementary level, the intermediate class becomes intimidating. When you skip simple fractions and jump into complex fractions, the only thing you will get is frustration. Many detest the subject because they are not always willing to go through the process and think through the steps to solving the problem. If you follow the step-by-step process of solving a mathematical problem, it is always easy to identify where you missed it in the process. This is very important if you do not want to make the same mistake again.

We give up often because we don't want to follow the process required to actualize our goals in life. The source of failure and frustration for many is in making the same mistake over and over and not being able to identify the specifics of the error. Experience earned from mistakes, if they help you recognize and learn, is a treasure. You cannot claim expertise in an area where you continue to commit the same error without the ability to resolve it. The resolution of your mistakes lies in the ability to identify what caused you to fail. You can never avoid a pitfall you are unable to identify. You also need to have an ongoing process of evaluation in place. This will provide you an opportunity to monitor the progress of your efforts and make adjustments as needed until you see the desired fruit or result.

A quality seed planted on a wrong soil has many options—it can die due to lack of nutrients, remain alive but dormant, or attempt to grow among thorns and thistles and be choked out of life. That seed can never produce at the level of its potential until you plant it on the right soil. Likewise, a perverse seed on a fertile soil can never bring forth quality fruit.

A seed can only produce after its kind regardless of the richness of the soil.

Planting season has its peculiar challenges. You are never going to be in absolute control of the yield, which can sometimes make you feel unmotivated. You are not in control of the weather. Not every idea can thrive in every climate. Some predators may want to eat up your harvest before it is ripe. Be prepared to keep them at bay. The solution to getting yourself prepared up for the challenge of the season is understanding that nothing you are aiming at now hasn't been done before. If you are humble enough to learn from the people who have done it before you, you will be at an advantage by avoiding the pitfalls that hindered or delayed them in their pursuit. Learn from people who have failed. You learn more from failures than success if you are wise enough not to repeat the same mistakes.

Planting is very diverse and specific to each aspect of life. For instance, the quality of your health is a product of the kind of lifestyle you have embraced. If you keep planting junk foods, fatty foods, and inactivity in your body, very soon, the harvest will come in the form of ill health. A nursing instructor once said nurses will never be jobless as long as people continue to smoke, eat foods that clog their arteries, and live a sedentary life. Some of your health issues are products of what you plant in your body.

Whatever you are planting in your children today will determine the type of adults they will become. Always remember that the harvest is more than the seed planted. If you sow evil, you will reap evil in multiple folds. If you plant goodness, goodness will come back to you in abundance. Plant daily, not for your own benefit alone but for humanity. Mother Teresa showed kindness not because she wanted to be popular but to make a difference. Her seed of good deeds earned her an immortal status after her demise; she lives on because her memory, based on the seed she planted for the good of humanity, became a point of reference.

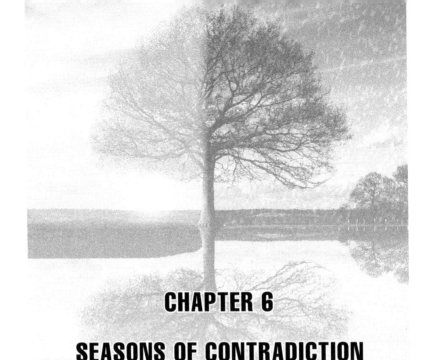

CHAPTER 6

SEASONS OF CONTRADICTION

The first and most important way of dealing with any problem is to acknowledge that it exists.

So, you have prepared for life and strategically planted quality seed on good soil. What do you do when the yield is not congruent with your sacrifices? How do you handle life when it hits you on the blind side? How do you reconcile a loss you did not anticipate? What do you do when the future you have envisioned quietly vanishes? What do you do when the place that once made you secure suddenly becomes a threat to your security? What do you do when the relationship that once brought you joy becomes the source of anguish? How do you deal with being bitten by the mouth you once fed? Life sometimes gets contradictory, and contradictions are inescapable. They are part of life and often comes when you least expect them. It does not matter what you have done right or wrong. You will have to deal with seasons of contradictions, and unfortunately, you may not be able to decide or influence the type of contradictions you will have to deal with and the people that will be the cause of your life issues. Most of the time, critical issues that tend to break people's hearts arise from family members and close allies.

This season is the most rewarding for people who have an understanding of life and the transient nature of each season. You have the opportunity to grow and become a better person. If not handled well, the season can leave you stranded and make you bitter for life. Many people have committed suicide or have been victims of homicide because of inability to deal with life's inevitable pressure and contradictions. When Kate Spade, Robin William, and Anthony Bourdain committed suicide around the same time, many people wondered why such notable people of influence and affluence, who appeared to have access to resources that most people couldn't dream of, could take their own life. The answer simply was the inability to deal with life's pressure in an area of life that seemed important to them. Societal status does not exonerate anyone from life's pressure. It becomes difficult and complicated to handle issues if you can cover up and pretend everything is fine. Public life often puts people in a compromising situation, especially when the nature of your job requires that you act in a way to maintain professionalism and job etiquette. Most people do not have a life-work balance, and this complicates the ability to deal with contradictions when they arise. The first and most important way of dealing with any problem is to acknowledge that it exists.

You can never change what you cannot confront.

You need to get to the point of accepting that you will have to deal with contradictions in life, no matter how good intentioned you are. If you are yet to experience failure, setbacks, betrayal, disappointment, tragedy, or situations that will attempt to break you, then you have not experienced life. Deep life experience may not leave any noticeable scar on your body, but they do leave hidden scars on your heart if you are fortunate enough to get the wound to heal. It is crucial that you find a way to determine the source of your problems. Inability to identify the source, or root cause, of your issue may leave you with managing symptoms and can only give you temporary relief.

In working with patients, I have realized that depression is a symptom and not necessarily a diagnosis. Some of the root causes of the symptoms of depression are generally not related to medical issues. They often have to do with emotional and psychological issues that patients do not want to discuss if they don't feel safe or comfortable enough to make themselves vulnerable. The problem will always resurface and probably worsen if the root cause is left unidentified and unaddressed. Identifying the root cause will help you come to terms with reality, since things are not always the way they appear. The contradictions in your life might have originated from a relationship or an association with a manipulative person who always makes you feel that you are the problem. Attempting to address an issue that is unreal may sap your energy. You may end up trying to fix yourself by compromising your dreams, principles, and values. You will eventually end up confused and frustrated when all your efforts failed to yield any resolution, and there will be no resolution because your interventions cannot address the real problem. Your ability to determine the source of your dilemma helps to keep you sane even in a situation beyond your control.

Pay attention to people who always blame others for their deeds. They often know how to get out of trouble by dumping the responsibility of their actions on others. If you have such an individual in your life, your experience will always be a vicious circle of traumatic events. Failure to deal with this type of relationship can cost you more than you can afford to part with. Dealing with it may also put you in a compromising situation depending on the kind of relationship and how much equity you have built over time with the individual or organization. Never make a permanent change to anything until you have carefully done a risk analysis. Depending on the odds against you or what may be at stake, having conversations about your concerns may be all that is needed to deal with the issues and get a lasting resolution. At times, you may need to set new boundaries and accountability structure to redefine how things ought to play out. Other times, the only option may be to run for your life, especially if your health and wellbeing are on the line. There is no one-size-fits-all when dealing with life issues. The uniqueness of your life and the peculiarities of people involved will determine the approach.

Sometimes the source of your contradictions may be linked to your childhood and the habits you formed in your early years. The habits you formed will eventually form you; they become your character and your personality. Negative habits lead to flawed character, and some of the character flaws may be the reason for your problems on the job or relationships with others. In my dealings with people as a manager, I have come to terms with the reality that you can only train people with the skills to do the job, but you can never change their character. I have worked with highly-skilled, intelligent people who are misfits for the organization and couldn't keep their job because of their flawed personality. The common thing I have identified with some of these people is their lack of awareness of the flaws and inability to take ownership of results. They act as if they are being victimized and often blame others for their woes. If you notice a pattern of challenges in your life that you have had to blame others for, you may need to do a soul searching and discover what is precipitating the reactions you are getting from people. If the problem is a result of a flawed character that was a norm due to your upbringing, discovering the abnormality in your normal is the first step to solving your crisis.

Nothing will change until you change. You will continue to flip jobs and relationships if you do not make a conscious effort to replace the old habits and flawed character traits with new habits and traits. You have people who are beautiful pathological liars and will lie about things that make you wonder if they have a soul. Beware of people with selective memory. They are likely covering something up. Character flaws are often the source of adversity in people's lives. It's always good to look inward and criticize yourself. If you are to be a hiring manager, will you hire someone with your type of character or work ethic? Would you be comfortable if your son or daughter married someone like you? Would you appreciate people managing your business the way you are operating your employer's business?

The most difficult contradictions in life are those that are difficult to blame on anything or anyone. They are like storms in life that happens naturally and hit everyone and everything in its path. <u>Storms of life can be difficult to comprehend and impossible to explain.</u> All you can do is accept them and find victory in your defeat. For people with understanding, there are always victories in every defeat. It takes a matured mind to grasp this depth and accept failure as a rudiment for success. Failure is a vital component of life that allows for the birthing of great destiny.

> *Failure is profitable if you do not fail to learn from the failure.*

Inability to learn life lessons from your failure puts you in a vicious cycle of error or tragic experience in life. Someone once asked Bill Gates the secret of his success, and he cited the managers he employed to run the operations. When asked about his selection criteria, he told the interviewer that there is a question that determines the overall selection. If they have a history of failure, then they have what it takes to succeed. What a contradiction! If they claim to have only experienced success, with no failure, then there is no room for them on his team.

Music is something that feeds my soul. In my highs and lows, I always find a song that speaks to my situation. One day, I was listening to this song. It is well with my soul, and the lyrics aroused my curiosity. Of course, that wasn't my first time listening to or singing the song, but that was the first time I could connect with the meaning, and so I did a little research on how the song came about, and my finding is worth sharing in this book. That song was written over one hundred years ago, and yet it is still so relevant today, because it was birthed in adversity.

Horatio G. Spafford was a successful lawyer and businessman in Chicago with a wife and five children. One of the children died in 1871 from pneumonia complications, and in the same year, they lost their business in the firestorm at Chicago. They recovered, and the business blossom again. On November 21, 1873, Mrs. Spafford and the four remaining children took a trip to Europe with 313 other travelers through the French ocean liner, *Ville du Havre*, from the United States. After four days on the trip into the crossing of the Atlantic, their ship crashed with a Scottish ship. A total of 226 passengers died, including the four Spafford children. Mrs. Spafford was rescued by a sailor, rowing a small boat over the spot where the ship went down. They boarded another vessel, which took them to Cardiff, Wales. She sent a wired message to her husband from there, which read, "Saved alone. What shall I do?"

Mr. Spafford decided to take the next available ship so he could join his wife. Four days into the journey, the captain called him over to show him the spot of the event that took the lives of his four daughters. Bertha Spafford Vester, a daughter born after the accident, reported that Spafford wrote the song "It Is Well with My Soul" during the trip:

> When peace, like a river, attendeth my way,
> When sorrows like sea billows roll;
> Whatever my lot, Thou hast taught me to say,
> It is well; it is well with my soul.

The core of your being will always surface during rough seasons of life. Losing four children at the same time cannot be less than a tragedy, but the man has his name inscribed on the sand of time because of the adversity he survived and the way he handled it. At least, the song still has relevance after one hundred years. Life's contradictions and storms will expose your core strength. Storms of life will put you in survival mode. You have questions that nothing can provide you with a reasonable answer. Seasons of grief, loss, despair, and hopelessness are bound to surface in life. One definite assurance is that it is only a season. It will not last. The longest and darkest of the night can never prevent the day from breaking. Having this understanding helps you to persevere. The same way you cannot prevent or stop natural storms, there are life storms that you may not be able to avoid.

Life's tempests can take many different forms—ill health despite conscious efforts to do the right thing, broken relationship, rebellious children, financial and economic hardship, addiction, and much more. It is essential to have a list of "what if's" in life. It helps you put things in proper perspective and have a game plan for eventualities. This is not negative thinking; I will call it "emergency preparedness for life."

1. What if my health fails? Do I have a plan?
2. What if I go bankrupt or lose all my investments? Do I have a plan to keep my body and soul together while I rebuild?
3. What if the career I built for twenty-five years loses its relevance? Do I have a plan?
4. What if the man (or woman) I plan to marry calls off the wedding? Can I deal with it?
5. What if my spouse dies and I have always been a stay-at-home mom? Can I adjust to my new reality?
6. What if my wife dies during childbirth? Can I deal with it?

7. What if my plan fails? Do I have a plan?
8. What if there is an outbreak of war or a terrorist attack? Do I have a plan?

The "what ifs" of life are endless, but the few I have listed have happened to people I knew before, and they were able to handle the situation and recover. The most important plan is to maintain a steady mindset that will not give up or faint in the face of adversity or tragedy. <u>If your mind is not resolute on survival, you will not be able to implement any other plan.</u> People who end up committing suicide do so because they can't see beyond their dark season. You can always find a way out, no matter how difficult the situation is. A bend in the road is not the end of the road. You can turn your stumbling blocks to stepping stones. There is the need for you to have a life jacket that will keep you afloat when the sea rolls and you experience a shipwreck in life. You may not need the lifejacket on every voyage; however, you cannot predict when you will need one. You can anticipate a storm, but it's difficult to predict its severity.

> *If you fall to pieces in a crisis, there wasn't much to you in the first place.*
> —*King Solomon*

Storms of life do have their benefits. Here are some fundamental facts about life's storms:

1. Storms are inevitable. They are natural.
2. They are temporary; no hurricane, cyclone, earthquake, or typhoon is indefinite.

3. Storms are always moving. You don't need to run away from the tempest if you have a "shelter in the storm," since the storm will eventually pass.
4. Storms force change. Life's storms will force you to change your lifestyle and choices.
5. Storms restore nature to its original state. Storms will help you find or discover your core strength.
6. Storms bring out everything hidden on its path and test the foundation. It will expose your weaknesses and confirm how strong you are.
7. Storms cleanse the environment and remove pollution.

Your situation is not the worst. I heard the story of a man who had a pair of shoes and was unhappy until he met a man without shoes. The man without shoes thought he had the worst situation until he met a man without feet. The man without feet felt his case was the worst until he encountered a dead body. As long as you have life, never write yourself off based on your experience.

What to do in the face of life's adversity:

1. Take time to count your blessings. When you look inward and do a soul-searching, you will find something no matter how insignificant that is good about your life. Focus on the good and appreciate the little blessings. It helps you to garner strength and build hope.
2. Change your perspectives. Some of life's disappointments stem from unmet expectations. Reprioritizing your priorities will help you focus on things that are realistic and help you divert your resources and energy on things that are profitable.

3. Find yourself. Your core values and guiding principles will help you in this season. If you don't have guiding principles that form the underpinnings of your life, you may be at the mercy of life's events.

4. Do something that will fill your cup—pray, sing a song, journal your thoughts, write a book, read, attend concerts. Music is a powerful food for the soul. Go mountain climbing. Go to the beach. Travel. Travel is therapeutic. It gives you a new outlook on things.

5. Don't try to hold on anything the storm is trying to take away, or else the storm will take you along.

6. Don't put an end to your story, by committing suicide or homicide.

7. Don't put your life on hold or give up pursuing your purpose. You may need to change your course. Never change your destination because of a diversion, unless the new destination offers a better opportunity.

8. Identify your anchor. If you don't have an anchor before the storm, it may be a chaotic experience. Learn to identify and reach out to people who have an anchor to lend you a helping hand. Find a support system. Some people are always willing to help with no strings attached. I love the song "Lean on Me," whose lines include, "Please swallow your pride if I have things you need to borrow, for no one can fill those of your needs that you won't let show." You can't live a solo life, but you also don't need the whole neighborhood in your business.

9. Avoid a pity party. The only thing it will offer you is depression.

10. Appreciate people who will tell you the truth when it hurts. It helps you to take ownership and responsibility. Tough times don't last, and as you persevere through the night, the day will break.

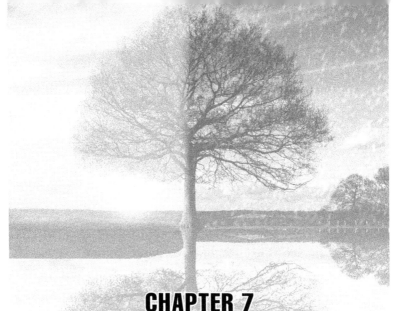

CHAPTER 7

SEASONS OF FLOURISHING

Receiving and retaining life's bounties require skill and tact.

To the average person, the season of flourishing may appear as the best and most profitable season of life, but to people who have understanding, it is the most delicate of all the seasons. Life presents everyone with opportunities to become better; however, people's expectation of flourishing sometimes is something free that requires no effort. Receiving and retaining life's bounties require skill and tact. Lack of understanding can be a liability during this time of life. Everyone has limitations based on what they know as a result of information at their disposal. Understanding, which is your ability to comprehend information, is an asset if you desire to flourish. Information and comprehension without application puts you in the same category as people who are completely ignorant. Your ability to secure lucrative employment after graduation, which is a form of flourishing in your career pursuit, is not enough. You need to have what it takes to perform and to grow.

In my experience as a hiring manager, I have seen many people remain in the same spot despite the potential for advancement because they became complacent and failed to create the capacity needed for continuous growth. A garden you fail to maintain will eventually lose its beauty and become a bush. A bush has everything that is needed to be a beautiful garden except a commitment from someone to keep pruning and tilling the ground on an ongoing basis. Flourishing requires a lot of energy and focus for its sustainability. This time puts you in control and command of life's resources and events, yet it can land you in grief if you are not equipped to handle the opportunities well.

During this time, you have "access" to opportunities in life. It's one thing to *have access* to opportunities; it's another thing to see and utilize the opportunities. Membership privileges can only grant you access to perks. Utilizing them, which requires time and commitment, is your responsibility—and you either use it or lose it. Registering with a fitness club is not enough to make you fit if you don't create the time to work out.

Many people take things for granted, thinking life's opportunities will always be at their beckoning. If you are not prepared with a plan in place before this season of your life, you may end up missing great things, people, and experiences. Sometimes this season may only present valuable relationships that you need to flourish, someone who will open your eyes of understanding to see things the way they are. Dependent and entitled people see harvest as labor. Harvesting requires diligence and focus, and if you don't have them, you will be at a disadvantage.

> *Diligent hands will rule, but laziness ends in forced labor.*
> —*King Solomon*

I was never privileged to have firsthand experience on a farm. However, lessons learned from farmers show that you can lose your harvest to pests or parasites if you are not diligent. The produce can become rotten if you fail to gather the crops at the right time. Harvest season presents with a surplus that might be wasted in the hand of unskilled people. Flourishing in life is not about the amount of money or possessions you can acquire. It has so much to do with how you can contain and preserve your acquisition, your actualized dreams, and your purpose. Many great destinies have been truncated at the prime of breakthrough due to inability to handle the season of flourishing. This season requires that you are active, proactive, and energetic.

Laziness is a killer. It's a busy time, and it's imperative you learn and know how to identify your priorities and prioritize them. Some things cannot wait; otherwise, they will become a waste. Windows of opportunity sometimes open just once in a lifetime, and only prepared minds can see and take advantage of them. Never postpone what you find convenient to do today. That business idea you are putting off may be all that you need to reach your next level. The difficult conversation you have been putting off may be all you need to get your sanity back and enjoy the blessings in your life without feelings of anger, hatred, or animosity.

> *Procrastination is the grave in which opportunities are buried.*
> —*Unknown author*

If the ant, without a leader or guide, understands the need to take advantage of the surplus and opportunities of summer to prepare for the scarcity and adversity of winter, then you have all you require to manage your season of flourishing.

This season requires focus, effort, and strategic thinking. Your skills at planning and planting are significant assets that can help you secure a lifetime harvest. You have access to quality seed; you can plant for your next level. If you are not proactive and strategic in the way you think, you can mismanage all the bounties of the season. A person with a consumerist mindset will never understand that this is the time of life to plan for adversity by taking advantage of the resources and relationships they have. Many have abused the platform for greatness presented to them through indiscretion. If you are a scoundrel, you can end up being completely messed up.

I followed the story of Bernard Madoff and the events that landed him with a jail term of 150 years. The man might not have intended to defraud his client. He was probably delivering results initially, which motivated the people to continue investing. His inability to sustain the harvest due to the lack of guiding principles, core values, and a strategic plan put him in a compromising situation. A person of integrity would have been upfront with the investors and stop promising what he could not deliver. Another lesson I garnered from his story was his lack of preparedness for true success. Anybody can efficiently manage failure, but success can be very challenging to manage. If you accidentally make it to the top, you have the tendencies of accidentally making it back down again. Then, when you fail, it will be difficult to pinpoint what went wrong and learn in a way to avoid similar pitfalls.

I taught high school mathematics for a while, and one key to understanding mathematical concepts is the need for a step-by-step approach in solving the questions. The process allows students to see where they missed the answer. Everything is cumulative and correcting a miscalculation that can be fixed in ten seconds can have a dramatic impact on the whole formula. If the student cannot show how they arrived at the answers, then they do not truly understand the concept. This applies to success in life. There is a process to follow. If you desire to flourish in your health, there are basic things you cannot do, like eat junk foods or maintain a sedentary lifestyle. Success comes with peculiar demands, and it takes a deliberate intention to meet the challenges that come with it.

Harvest in the hand of an unprepared mind can become rotten. If you do not expect good things, it does not matter whether valuable opportunities come your way; you will still not be able to receive and contain them. I read the story of a man, David Lee Edwards, who won a $27 million jackpot in 2001. Within five years, he had lost everything. He could not handle the bounty life had put in his path, and upon his death twelve years after the win, there was no money left for his funeral. The unexpected riches thrown at him opened him up to reckless living that led to his premature death. He lived a life of fantasy for five years and went back to where he belonged, an impoverished mindset. People with ideas could have multiplied the $27 million. A man full of ideas will always flourish. Money is not synonymous with wealth. There is more to wealth than liquid cash. Show me a man with ideas, and I will show you a man with the potential to flourish in life. All the Wright Brothers had was an idea. The ideas of Steve Jobs, Thomas Edison, Karl Benz, and people of like minds are still flourishing after their demise—that is real wealth. Most people who got rich by chance without the discovery of purpose and understanding of economics always end up being destroyed by the unexpected riches through drugs, prostitution, alcoholism, gambling, and all sorts of unhealthy choices.

> *Access to money in the absence of ideas will eventually lead to poverty.*

Life's opportunities sometimes come like drops of mercy, but people always look for showers. When you take advantage of the little drops, you can build a pool, and if you are in the midst of a heavy downpour of rain with no strategic plan, you will end up in a drought when the showers of rain cease. The job you have now may be the platform you need for your next level. Unfortunately, if you don't see the blessings in the position, you may end up focusing on amplifying the negatives. This will hamper you from taking advantage of available resources that you can use as a ladder to get something bigger and better.

As I stated earlier, the man behind the strategic thinking, planning, and implementation of the solution to the first global economic crisis reported in human history did so at a time when the economy was flourishing in Egypt. It would have been practically impossible to salvage the economic meltdown if Joseph did not have the understanding of handling the season of abundance. He had an understanding of the transient nature of seasons and knew how to preserve the season of flourishing in a way that when that season lapsed and gave way to a season of global recession, there was a provision for relief enough to sustain the whole world. His strategic plan turned his country of naturalization to the wealthiest nation of his time. They had the monopoly of the world food market in a way that no other government could match. Understanding of life's seasons will give you a sense of direction and put you in command.

Understanding will always make you outstanding.

In your quest for survival and acquisition of the numerous bounties presented on the table of life, please acquire understanding.

What you fail to understand will put you under.

When you bring children into the world without the understanding of the responsibilities of parenting, you are bound to face a crisis. You will always be frustrated in areas of life where you lack understanding. The precursor to understanding is knowledge. I am not talking about earning a college degree. There are ignorant degree holders who think they know everything needed for life but are confused. Their life choices are evidence of the depth of their confusion. A prideful individual can never learn, and when you do things the same way you have always done them, you will only get the results you have always gotten.

Ignorance can have a negative impact on this season. I have addressed the issue of the mindset and still need to reinforce it again. Your mindset sets your life's limits, irrespective of the accessibility to opportunities. What your mind cannot conceive, your hand cannot receive.

I met with a lady who needed some guidance. After she enumerated all her issues, I suggested she prioritize her issues and tackle them one at a time. She was working as a cleaner in a restaurant. She seemed excited about the job due to previous laborious work she had had to do in the past. Assessing her situation, I saw much potential and offered to help her get a better job that would pay her 50 percent more than she was making. Her new environment would challenge her thinking, and she would receive a full benefits package, including tuition assistance. I reached out to someone who was willing to create the position based on my referral. As soon as the recruiter reached out to the lady, she sent me a message to appreciate my effort and her unwillingness to part with her current status. According to her, one of the best things in her life was that job. She could not imagine any place better than her current employment. She complained about how life had been cruel to her but failed to realize that sometimes what you put into life determines what you get out of life. A window of opportunity opened up to her, and she shut it because she could not see beyond the now.

What is your life's vision? If you experience the season of flourishing in life without a vision, you will end up a spectator. I spoke extensively on vision in my book *Leadership Extraordinaire*. The need for insight and foresight in life are not negotiable for someone who desires to become accomplished and fulfilled. People without foresight lives for now, as if there were no tomorrow. Where do you see yourself after now? What if the plenty you have now become extinct? Vision puts you on the platform of greatness and keeps you there. If life dropped its bounty on your path right now, would you recognize it? You can't handle what you fail to recognize. Many are looking at the harvest of opportunities right under their nose, but they can't see it.

The entire nation of Zambia was being governed by a bunch of visionless people with no insight, foresight, or oversight. They decided to sell the country's harvest of mined copper for $400 million. The company negotiated to pay $25 million in cash and use $375 million to make up for the depreciation of the equipment. Bottom line: the copper mine was sold for $25 million and a royalty of 0.06%. The company has consistently been making $500 million on an annual basis.

Before you judge the foolishness of so-called leaders, please look inward and ask yourself a sincere question: what aspect of my life have I voluntarily handed over to people for free, and they are making a fortune out of it because I do not understand my worth? They are milking you, and all you get in return is a peanut.

> *The only thing worse than being blind is having sight but no vision.*
> —Helen Keller

Besides vision, other virtues will help you thrive and sustain your season of flourishing. As you experience the season of flourishing, you need discipline. Never say yes to an offer that is alien to your guiding principles and core values. It may be a distraction to lure you away from focus and what is essential. You stand the chance of facing various temptations. The season may bring with it an opportunity for you to be popular. Always understand that most of the people who gravitate toward you during this season are only doing so because of your fruits and what they can get from you. The moment you become fruitless, don't be surprised if so-called friends and acquaintances decide to abandon you.

It is essential that you have a system of accountability in place. You may need more than one, depending on the different areas of your life that are blossoming at the same time. These people should be comfortable enough to tell you as it is. They may be younger or older than you; however, they need to be brutally honest with you. People like this are rare, but they do exist. Find someone who can tell you the truth even when it hurts. Never allow this season to put you in a position where you cannot be corrected. Stubbornness can be very destructive. You will need to make room for some flexibility without compromising your purpose, principles, and values. Your depreciation starts the day you cannot be corrected. Don't surround yourself with "yes people" who are only after what they can benefit from you.

> *People who come to your life because of gain will eventually leave you in pain when there is nothing to gain.*

Another pitfall to avoid during this time of life are personal habits that are detrimental to the sustainability of your success. They may be minute or insignificant but can be disastrous over time. Most scandals in life come during this season as a result of bad habits that you fail to deal with during the season of preparation. For instance, if you are building a life that requires a public platform, you must deal with certain things before ascending the platform of your expression. You will always face opposition, no matter how well-intentioned you are. Bad habits in your life give your opponents the ammunition to wage war against you. Many people have been hindered and disqualified from the bounties of life in the prime of their career and endeavors, not because of incompetence but because of lack of discipline.

> *Everyone must choose one of two pains: the pain of discipline or the pain of regret.*
> —Jim Rohn

Contentment is another pitfall during this season. This is a must-have virtue which can become a hindrance in the hand of lazy people. Never hide behind the notion of being content in life to the point of becoming obsolete. Whatever you are doing now is no longer a potential. You need to challenge yourself and reach for something higher and better. Please understand that complacency will only put you behind time. We are in a world that is continuously evolving. Nothing in life is static; you need to continue to improve on yourself. Learning should be a lifetime adventure.

You can never achieve success in a silo. Recognize the active and passive contributors to your achievements. Identify factors, people, and systems that help sustain your growth and those that can potentially bring you down. Many factors will determine the sustenance of your season of flourishing.

The story of Blockbuster, a one-time leader in the movie rental business, is a relevant one to share. The company entered a season of flourishing that put them at the pinnacle of success. Unfortunately, they failed to pay attention to the evolution of technology, which presented a subtle, indirect competition for their business. When Netflix, a not-so-important competitor in the movie rental business, approached them for a partnership deal, they declined the offer. Reed Hastings, founder of Netflix, had a foresight of the potential benefit of technological advancement to build an online brand. He saw a company that could operate with reduced overhead cost through the elimination of the operating expense of a traditional movie rental business. Declining that deal led to the extinction of Blockbuster. Leadership couldn't see beyond generating revenue by taking advantage of the customers through late fees and membership fees.

There is always a better way of getting things done. The strategy that worked today may not work tomorrow. You need to keep up at improving yourself and your business strategies, even in the face of obvious success, and never get to a point of taking things for granted, especially when things are good. The pain of loss of a pleasant or valuable thing, investment, relationship, or experience is deep. It is worse when the memory reminds you of missed opportunities on things you could have done to save the day. It is impossible to mourn the loss of a thing you never had, since there is no memory or reference point, which makes this season a delicate period of life.

It is not uncommon for people to commit suicide in the face of loss or threat of imminent loss. I read an article published on the *Forbes* on June 12, 2014, reporting the results of a research conducted by the University of Oxford on economic suicides. Across the US, Europe, and Canada between 2008 and 2010, about 10,000 suicides were linked to economic downturn, with risk factors of job loss, foreclosure, and debt. The same research shows no increase in suicide in other countries, like Sweden and Austria, despite the same level of economic downturn. The disparity demonstrates that the loss of money or possessions is not enough to cause loss of life as long as there is an understanding of how life works and a reasonable system of support. Life is a process, and if there is a true understanding of life's seasons, you can survive the most seemingly impossible situation and also effectively manage the abundance that crosses your path without losing your mind.

CONCLUSION

Life is not a problem to be solved but a reality to be experienced.

—*Soren Kierkegaard*

As I conclude, it's important to highlight few key points of wisdom. Change is the most constant event in life. Time changes everything. When you understand life as a season, you will easily persevere during seasons of unpleasant realities and avoid taking things for granted when things are in your favor. Life is like a puzzle. It cannot make sense until everything is put together, so don't judge your life based on a piece. It will never make any sense, so don't give up until the whole puzzle is put together. Your perspective about life will always shape your experience in life. If you see problems, you will be overwhelmed, but if you see opportunities, you will be motivated. There are things in life you will not be able to change. Learn to accept your realities. Your mind is the greatest asset or liability that can help you win or lose in life. No one has it all together, but people with togetherness have it all. You will need the help of others at some point. The need to learn from others how to navigate your way through life is one you cannot afford to compromise.

Time management, your greatest treasure, and the concept of choice are building blocks of a meaningful life. You are the only one that can choose the outcome of your life. It is yours to own. It will always be difficult for people to look up to you when you look down on yourself. The value people will place on you depends on how you view yourself. Accepting your uniqueness and celebrating your authentic self is the gateway to a life of fulfillment.

The seasons of life cannot damage an individual who has discovered his worth. Every situation is transient. Bad tends to become worse, and good can become better, so complacency or indifference will make you lose at your game.

Good things happen to bad people, and bad things happen to good people. Sometimes it is not what you have done right or wrong. Harvest is a function of seed planted. You will always determine the quality of your harvest based on the quality of your seed. Storms are natural. You may not be able to prevent them, but you have all you need to identify and run to a shelter. There is always a shelter in the storm.

OTHER BOOKS BY THE AUTHOR:

 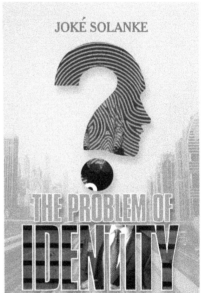

Contact the author at:

web: blossomlifeoutreach.com
Email: blossomlifeoutreach@gmail.com

CPSIA information can be obtained
at www.ICGtesting.com
Printed in the USA
BVHW080935180319
542953BV00011B/278/P